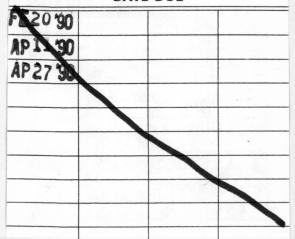

BUREAUCRACY ON TRIAL

Policy Making by Government Agencies

AN ADVANCED STUDY IN POLITICAL SCIENCE

BUREAUCRACY
ON TRIAL
✳✳✳

Policy Making by
Government Agencies

William W. Boyer
UNIVERSITY OF PITTSBURGH

THE BOBBS-MERRILL COMPANY, INC.
A SUBSIDIARY OF HOWARD W. SAMS & CO., INC.
Publishers · INDIANAPOLIS · NEW YORK · KANSAS CITY

ROBERT C. WOOD, Consulting Editor

The Massachusetts Institute of Technology

TO DAVID FELLMAN

Preface

Only in the United States is "bureaucracy" an ugly word. Yet, curiously, the same persons and interests who complain about bureaucracy are those who by their demands on government help to make it grow. The framers of our institutions did not anticipate these developments, and increasingly the perennial question of liberty versus authority is becoming an issue of bureaucracy versus democracy.

This book is, essentially, an analysis of decision making in administrative agencies—of the making of agency policies that affect private rights and interests against a setting of multiple and powerful pressures. Policy making by legislatures, by courts, and by chief executives and politicians have all received their fair share of attention from scholars, journalists, and others. But policy making by government agencies is still practically virgin territory for the scholar.

To be sure, there have been antibureaucracy tirades; some respectable legal studies of administrative adjudication and analyses of national regulation, most of which have concentrated on the few federal regulatory commissions; a growing number of interdisciplinary studies of organization generally; and a host of case studies. But where are the comprehensive studies of policy making by government agencies that seek an understanding of the totality rather than of one or another of its parts?

In posing the question, I have stated the purpose of the book. But I hasten to add that I make no bold claims. Mine is an attempt to make a beginning toward filling the void of comprehensive analysis. The subject is vast and merits a grand effort of many scholars for many years to come. This book not only attempts a general description and analysis of policy making in administrative agencies but is also concerned with administrative policy making in terms of its relation to democratic government and "due process." I readily acknowledge the limitations of this work; I beckon other social scientists to follow my effort, to broaden their vision and concern, to join in the search for improvements in our system of public administration, and thereby to enrich our living and safeguard our liberties.

This book had its genesis in 1953 when Orrin L. Helstad, now professor of law at the University of Wisconsin, and I were retained by the Wisconsin Legislative Council to make a study of the rule-making procedures of seventy-one Wisconsin administrative agencies. I am indebted to Professor Helstad for much of my understanding of the administrative process. I wish also to express my gratitude to Earl Sachse, executive secretary of the Council; to Walter J. Kohler, former governor of Wisconsin, whom it was my privilege to serve as administrative assistant subsequent to the Council study; to Edward H. Litchfield, chancellor of the University of Pittsburgh, and Holbert N. Carroll, chairman of that university's Department of Political Science, for creating the institutional conditions that made possible the preparation of this volume; to James D. Thompson, former director of the University of Pittsburgh's Administrative Science Center, for many invaluable suggestions; and to political scientists Frederick N. Cleaveland of the University of North Carolina and Robert C. Wood of The Massachusetts Institute of Technology, who read the entire manuscript and offered equally valuable suggestions.

I have benefited from the criticisms and suggestions of Donald E. Boles, of Iowa State University; Charles E. Redfield, management consultant; Earle P. Shoub, of the U.S. Bureau of Mines; and my colleagues at the University of Pittsburgh—Edward F. Cooke, Thomas M. Cooley II, Bela Gold, Morris Ogul, Joseph Pois, and Arthur Tuden. To them, I record my appreciation, as I do to the staffs of the University of Pittsburgh's Administrative Science Center, Public Affairs Library, and General Library for their assistance; to my many questioning students over the years; to many associates among government administrators at all levels, who have deepened my perspective; to Mrs. Ann Walko and Barbara Moll for exceptionally competent typing; and to Theodore Galovich, my former graduate assistant, who checked citations and otherwise saved me many hours.

The substance of portions of this work has appeared in two articles: "Legislative Controls of Administrative Rulemaking," *The American Bar Association Journal*, November 1955, co-authored with Orrin L. Helstad; and "Policy Making by Government Agencies," *The Midwest Journal of Political Science*, August 1960. I am grateful to the editors of these journals for permission to utilize this material in the revised form in which it appears here, and to Orrin L. Helstad for permission to draw from the studies upon which we worked together.

Finally, I am indebted to my wife for her forbearance and encouragement, and to others I shall not name. I, alone, am responsible for all deficiencies of this book.

WILLIAM W. BOYER

Pittsburgh, Pennsylvania
May 1964

Contents

PART ONE
THE PROCESS OF POLICY MAKING

PART TWO

PROBLEMS OF POLICY CONTROL

PART THREE

BUREAUCRACY AND DEMOCRACY

Introduction

Bureaucracy is on trial in the United States precisely because Americans are bound in countless ways by a vast array of rules and regulations made by an army of appointed administrators rather than by elected representatives of the people.

One of every seven employed Americans is employed by a government agency. Millions more produce for, and are financed by, government agencies. And all are regulated by them and pay substantially for the privilege.

Policies made and enforced by administrative agencies of government constitute, in large part, a body of law—usually called rules, regulations, or general orders—which public administrators promulgate or execute within authority delegated to them by legislatures. The term "policies," as used in this book, refers to agency statements, essentially legislative in substance, that affect private rights and interests.

When legislatures make laws, formally at least a prescribed procedure is followed, the major steps of which are broadly predictable. No parallel exists in the administrative process to govern the making of agency policies that have the force of law.

How do agencies make such policies? From what sources do administrators draw their ideas for policies? Are members of the public involved? Should they be? How do, and how should, administrators make known to citizens the rules and regulations that affect them? Within administrative policy making, are judicial and legislative procedures clearly distinguishable or hopelessly confused? What effective external controls may be imposed on administrative policy making that will not impair the administrative process? These and other questions treated in the following pages impinge on the basic issue of whether bureaucracy and democracy can coexist.

IMPORTANCE OF ADMINISTRATIVE POLICIES

The outstanding legal development in this century has been the growth of government policies made by numerous administrative agencies. Commenting on this development, Harrison Brown has written:

> As our population grows, as the pressures from outside become even more intense, as our industrial network becomes increasingly complex, as the problems of military defense become even more involved, we as a democratic society will be confronted internally by extraordinarily difficult problems. We have only seen the beginning of rules and regulations designed to bind men's actions. As time goes by, the people of the United States will be steadily driven toward increased organization, increased conformity and increased control over the thoughts and actions of the individual.[1]

Administrative policies already have an impact upon practically every human endeavor. They prescribe individual, group, and insti-

1 Harrison Brown, "The Prospective Environment for Policy Making and Administration," in Committee on Foreign Relations, United States Senate, *United States Foreign Policy, Compilation of Studies* (87th Cong., 1st sess., document 24) (Washington, D. C.: U. S. Gov't. Printing Office, March 15, 1961), p. 959. See the definitions of rule making and the distinctions between rule making and adjudication in: U. S. Department of Justice, *Attorney General's Manual on the Administrative Procedure Act* (Leavenworth, Kans.: Federal Prison Industries Inc. Press, 1947), p. 14; Kenneth C. Davis, *Administrative Law and Government* (St. Paul, Minn.: West Publishing Co., 1960), p. 117; and Ralph F. Fuchs, "Procedure in Administrative Rule Making," *Harvard Law Review*, LII (December 1938), 259-80, especially p. 265.

tutional behavior. They have the force of law. Their violation incurs loss of government services or benefits, or the imposition of sanctions.

The average citizen, both in his daily life and over his total life span, is affected intimately and continuously by the action of government administrative agencies. Administrative agencies, for example, impose requirements certifying compliance with government policies at the most meaningful milestones of the life process: the birth of a child; his graduation from the public schools; his marriage; and, finally, his death.

A typical day in the life of an average person illustrates the importance of administrative policies. If he drives his car to work, it is probably equipped and maintained to satisfy minimum requirements and specifications as determined by an administrative agency. His car is insured by a company regulated by an administrative agency. He must abide by administratively created traffic regulations involving such matters as speed zones and stop signs. If he should travel by bus, trolley, or railway, he must pay a fare fixed by a regulatory agency.

If he works in an office building, he probably ascends to his office in an elevator constructed and maintained in accordance with an administrative code. The building itself was probably planned by a licensed architect and constructed under the supervision of registered engineers pursuant to the administrative regulations of a building code; it was wired as prescribed by an electrical code, heated and ventilated according to another code, and equipped and fitted with plumbing fixtures as required by a plumbing code. He lunches at a restaurant where the equipment complies with health rules. The food he eats was produced and marketed under agricultural regulations, transported by means of regulated carriers, and processed according to administrative food standards.

These are only a few of the many examples that could be cited to illustrate the substantive impact of administrative policies on the life of the average citizen, who, most of the time, is not even conscious of their effect. The omnipresence of administrative policies is felt more keenly, of course, by various economic interest groups—trades, professions, and industries, for example—that are subject to their direct application.

RESORT TO THE ADMINISTRATIVE PROCESS

Congress, the state legislatures, and local legislative bodies have continuously and increasingly resorted to the administrative process for the formulation and application of public law. They have endowed administrative agencies with authority to determine or otherwise affect private rights, obligations, and interests by either rule or decision. The contemporary nature of this development is indicated by a 1941 report on fifty-two federal agencies granted such authority. The report reveals that thirty-five of the agencies were created during the first four decades of the twentieth century.[2] Other levels of government have had a similar experience. For example, a 1955 study found that, of forty-six Wisconsin agencies with rule-making or policy-making authority, thirty-six had been created since 1900.[3]

Legislatures have relied increasingly on the administrative process for a variety of reasons, and all these reasons have received much attention in the literature of public administration.[4] First among them is that government must respond promptly to many rapidly changing situations. Most legislatures in the United States meet only for

[2] Committee on Administrative Procedure, *Final Report of the Attorney General's Committee on Administrative Procedure* (Washington, D. C.: U. S. Gov't. Printing Office, 1941), pp. 9-10.

[3] Wisconsin Legislative Council, *Research Report on Administrative Rule Making—1955 Report* (Madison, Wisc.: State Capitol, 1954), pp. 4-6; cited hereafter as *1955 Report, Administrative Rule Making*. The term "agency" is used broadly to encompass a department, office, service, bureau, board, commission, corporation, authority, division, committee, or administration—to mention the usual appellations. In this study, an administrative agency means "an organ of government other than a court and other than a legislature, which affects the rights of private parties ..." (Kenneth C. Davis, *Administrative Law* [St. Paul, Minn.: West Publishing Co., 1951], p. 1). Agencies have "the power to determine ... private rights and obligations" (Committee on Administrative Procedure, *op. cit.*, p. 7).

[4] See, for example: Davis, *op. cit. supra*, note 1 at pp. 32-39; Committee on Administrative Procedure, *op. cit.*, pp. 11-18; James M. Landis, *The Administrative Process* (New Haven: Yale University Press, 1938), pp. 6-46; Edward L. Metzler, "The Growth and Development of Administrative Law," *Marquette Law Review*, XIX (June 1935), 209-27.

several months of every year, or only once every two years. But even
a legislature in continuous session is usually unable to act with celer-
ity in response to changing conditions. To secure the flexibility
necessary for effective governmental action, legislative bodies at all
levels have delegated to administrative agencies authority to deal
promptly with problems as they arise.

Sheer necessity is often the mother of delegation. A health agency,
for example, must have authority to act quickly to prevent an epi-
demic. A labor relations agency must be able in a timely fashion to
assure an equitable settlement to the parties of a labor dispute. A
securities agency should not have to wait for legislative clearance
before preventing a stock manipulation that would defraud the in-
vesting public.

A second, and most important, reason for resort to the administrative process is that the process permits and encourages the use of
specialists and experts. Every civilized society is confronted by increasingly complex economic and social problems. A basic purpose of
government is that of organizing society in such a manner as to assure
the security and welfare of its members. Legislatures alone cannot
provide this assurance in contemporary society. Economic and social
problems require the attention of those who have the time and facilities to remain continuously informed and specialized. Legislators
are not, and cannot be, expected to have expert knowledge in all the
areas in which they are compelled to act. For example, it is the function of the legislature to make the basic policy decision as to whether
a particular segment of the economy is to be regulated. But if the
field to be regulated is highly technical, expert knowledge is required.
It would be almost impossible for legislatures intelligently to fix the
rates that public utilities or insurance companies may charge. Consequently, legislators have devolved upon administrative agencies
authority to establish such rates, as well as to formulate safety codes,
building codes, food and drug standards, and health rules.

A third factor in the development of administrative policy making
is that as modern government has become big business, governmental
detail has grown to staggering proportions. The Attorney General's

Committee on Administrative Procedure commented on this in connection with congressional activities:

> Independently of the comparative advantages of administrative action, various inherent limitations upon its own functioning militate in these cases against action by Congress itself. The total time available is the most obvious. Time spent in details must be at the sacrifice of time spent on matters of broad public policy. . . . Even if Congress had the time and facilities to work out details, there would be constant danger of harmful rigidity if the result were crystallized in the form of a statute. Thus comes a steady pressure . . . to assign such tasks to the controlled discretion of some other agency.[5]

The great mass of detail for which administrative agencies are made responsible derives in large part from the trend toward preventive legislation, which usually takes the form of licensing—a means by which much government regulation is effected. There is little doubt that the time-consuming and detailed work required in licensing procedures can best be performed by administrative agencies. Neither legislatures nor courts are constituted to perform such functions, and where they have attempted to undertake licensing activities the insurmountable difficulties soon manifested themselves to all parties concerned.

Finally, federal grant-in-aid programs have stimulated state and local legislative bodies to resort to the administrative process, and such programs must be regarded as still another factor in the expansion of administrative regulation. Federal aid legislation generally requires the state or local government to designate an agency to be responsible for administering the program and for establishing necessary policies. For example, the Eighty-First Congress, in Public Law 734, provided that state plans for old age assistance and for aid to the blind and to the totally and permanently disabled must provide, "if the plan includes payments to individuals in private or public institutions, for the establishment or designation of a state authority or authorities which shall be responsible for establishing

[5] Committee on Administrative Procedure, *op. cit.*, p. 14.

and maintaining standards for such institutions."[6] State plans not in compliance with such federal mandates risk loss of federal aid.

THE DILEMMA FOR LEGISLATURES

Necessity, more often than not, has caused legislative bodies on the national, state, and local levels to delegate lawmaking authority to administrative agencies in spite of constitutional mandates stipulating that *all* legislative powers granted shall be vested in the legislature. The courts, in turn, have generally upheld this delegation of legislative authority to administrators if the legislature has fixed proper and clear standards to govern administrative discretion. But no amount of judicial exegesis or tortuous reasoning can obscure the evident fact that much of the legislative function has been transferred to the administrative process, and that a subtle but inexorable change has been effected in our system of government.

Legislatures increasingly have sensed a loss of control over the lawmaking function of government. The lobbyist, familiar with the legislative process, finds that traditional methods leave him unprepared to represent his interests in the formulation of administrative policies. The lawyer, trained in the traditional judicial process, often looks aghast at the highly complex and variegated administrative process. Indeed, much of this early opposition to the administrative process came from lawyers.[7]

Sharp attacks were made against the administrative process in its formative years. The reasoning employed was couched in questions such as these: Do these agencies not have authority to make policies that have the same force and effect as laws passed by the legislature? What, then, has happened to the fundamental principle that power to legislate cannot be delegated? Are not many administrators vested

---

[6] 64 U. S. Stat. 548 (1950).

[7] See Willard Hurst, *The Growth of American Law: The Law Makers* (Boston: Little, Brown and Company, 1950), pp. 400-11. See also Victor G. Rosenblum, "Realities of Regulation," *Public Administration Review*, XX (Autumn 1960), 219-27.

with authority to act as legislator, prosecutor, and judge? And is this not a violation of the principles of separation of powers and natural justice? Does not the growing pattern of administrative regulation undermine the ideal of representative government expressed through a popularly elected legislature, as well as the ideal of an independent and unbiased judiciary? Still another line of attack involved the charge that the administrative process did not provide adequate notice and opportunity for hearings, procedures that had come to be regarded as constituting an integral part of constitutional "due process of law."

Lawyers posed these same questions to the courts in terms of particular administrative programs. Each question attributed an evil to the administrative process. Many of the early attacks were aimed at destroying the administrative process rather than at improving it.

Challenges based on the theory of separation of powers have never yielded much success, nor have constitutional due process requirements noticeably impeded the growth of the administrative process. Though dissatisfaction with it has proved enduring, so has the need for its use. Accordingly, early attempts to destroy the administrative process were gradually replaced by efforts to devise means by which administrative procedure could be improved.

Meanwhile, the plight of the individual citizen becomes more apparent. The complexity of government only adds to his confusion. Faced with a legal problem, he is usually ignorant of the law. He feels that he cannot get through to the anonymous bureaucrat who makes decisions affecting him. Even his attorney cannot be certain of all the facets or requirements of the law. Perhaps an administrative agency has adopted and given force to a policy affecting the citizen. But a search of statute books and court decisions may reveal no authority for such a policy, and there may be no systematic publication of the rules and regulations of the agency. The policy or rule may exist only in the mind of the administrator, to be applied or not as he pleases. Little wonder, then, that many persons conclude that we are rapidly acquiring a government of men rather than a government of law.

Compounded, these many dissatisfactions with the administrative process spell a major dilemma for legislatures. It is within the usual powers of a legislature to check what it believes to be an abuse of administrative authority to make policies by utilizing one or more of the traditional control devices. The legislature can expressly repeal the policy in question. It can repeal the agency's authority to make the policy, or it can reduce the agency's appropriation. It can also deny approval of nominees for agency positions, or reorganize, abolish, or conduct an investigation of the agency.

The effectiveness of these techniques for control of specific policy making is questionable, however. Most of them are drastic remedies at best—hostile and retaliatory in character. Unless they are used judiciously, the purposes of delegation—the very reasons for resort to the administrative process—may be perverted or defeated. Except for a few extremists, those who have registered dissatisfaction with the administrative process have sought to promote legislative control of the process rather than to eliminate administrative programs or otherwise penalize administrative agencies.

Legislators, one can assume, do not want to impede administration unnecessarily. They recognize that the reasons for resort to the administrative process are valid. But they do want to recover their basic lawmaking function. They do want to be able to control the specific uses by administrative agencies of policy-making authority that they consider to be abused or unsound. That is why the traditional control devices have proved inadequate and new devices are being sought by legislatures.

The critical problem confronting legislatures is that of improving administrative procedure to assure democratic and responsible policy making without, at the same time, creating an administrative straitjacket or otherwise unduly hampering the administrative process. The problem is a basic one, fraught with considerations about our system of government and the nature of our state. In 1916, Elihu Root, then president of the American Bar Association, cautioned that

> . . . the powers that are committed to these regulating agencies, and which they must have to do their work, carry with them great and dangerous opportunities of oppression and wrong. If we are to continue a

government of limited powers these agencies of regulation must themselves be regulated. The limits of their power over the citizen must be fixed and determined. The rights of the citizen against them must be made plain. A system of administrative law must be developed, and that with us is still in its infancy, crude and imperfect.[8]

The basic question, then, is this: If lawmaking authority must be vested in an administrative agency, how can the legislature effectively control it? And what choices are available to the administrator, in the exercise of his policy-making discretion, that will facilitate the discharge of his responsibility to both the legislature and the public that is so necessary for the maintenance and practice of democratic administration?

THE REFORM MOVEMENT

Efforts to reform or improve administrative procedure began in England in 1929 with the publication of Lord Hewart's book *The New Despotism* and with the appointment of the Committee on Ministers' Powers. The committee was charged with the responsibility of recommending means by which the constitutional principles of the sovereignty of Parliament and the supremacy of law could be safeguarded against the encroachment of administrative agencies. It is noteworthy that the committee concluded in its famous report of 1932 that there was "no ground for public fear, if the right precautions are taken." The report was, in effect, a tribute to the administrative proc-

---

[8] Elihu Root, "Address of the President," *American Bar Association Journal*, II (October 1916), 736-55, at p. 750. Reporting on federal independent regulatory agencies in 1960, James M. Landis observed: "Their responsibility is to the Congress rather than solely to the Executive. The policies that they are supposed to pursue are those that have been delineated by the Congress not by the Executive. Departure from those policies or the failure to make them effective or their subordination of legislative goals to the directions of the Executive is thus a matter of necessary legislative concern. There is no question but that Congress has both the right and duty to inquire into effectiveness of the operation of the regulatory agencies and their handling of the broad powers that have been delegated to them. The real issue is the capacity of the Congress to keep abreast of the programs and the policies being carried out by these agencies" (James M. Landis, *Report on Regulatory Agencies to the President-Elect* [Washington, D. C.: U. S. Gov't. Printing Office, 1960], p. 34).

ess inasmuch as fifteen eminent people of diverse backgrounds could find nothing radically wrong with it.[9]

In the United States, significant advances in the movement for reform of administrative procedures have been registered nearly every year since 1932.[10] Annual reports on the subject were issued by the Special Committee on Administrative Law of the American Bar Association in 1933, 1934, 1935, and 1936. President Franklin D. Roosevelt appointed a Committee on Administrative Management in 1936 to study and report on "administrative methods, functioning, and organization." It was this committee which charged, in its 1937 report, that administrative agencies—particularly the independent regulatory commissions—had developed into a "fourth branch of the government," for which there was no sanction in the Constitution.[11]

Consequently, many bills were introduced in Congress allegedly aimed at effecting improvements in the practices and procedures of federal agencies. The most important of these was the Walter-Logan Bill, which was passed by Congress after prolonged hearings and debate.[12] However, this extreme measure prescribed a single, rigid procedure for all rule making, and its effect, as James M. Landis pointed out, would have been to "cut off here a foot and there a head, leaving broken and bleeding the processes of administrative law."[13] The bill

9 Committee on Ministers' Powers, *Report on Ministers' Powers* (London: His Majesty's Stationer's Office, 1932). See also Louis Jaffe, "Invective and Investigation in Administrative Law," *Harvard Law Review*, LII (June 1932), 1,201-1,245.

10 For more complete discussions of the reform movement in the United States, and for citations of the various studies, see Davis, *op. cit. supra*, note 1 at pp. 25-54, and E. Blythe Stason, "The Model State Administrative Procedure Act," *Iowa Law Review*, XXXIII (January 1948), 196-209. For surveys of comparable developments in representative states, see Ferrel Heady, *Administrative Procedure Legislation in the States* (Ann Arbor: Institute of Public Administration, University of Michigan, 1952), pp. 12-25, and Whitney R. Harris, "Administrative Practice and Procedure: Comparative State Legislation," *Oklahoma Law Review*, VI (February 1953), 29-64.

11 The President's Committee on Administrative Management, *Administrative Management in the Government of the United States* (Washington, D. C.: U. S. Gov't. Printing Office, 1937), p. 36.

12 H. R. 6324, 76th Cong., 3rd sess. (1939). For citations of literature provoked by this bill, see W. Brooke Graves, *Public Administration in a Democratic Society* (Boston: D. C. Heath & Co., 1950), p. 589, at note 17.

13 James M. Landis, "Crucial Issues in Administrative Law," *Harvard Law Review*, LIII (May 1940), 1,077-1,102.

was the product of the American Bar Association, which was conducting a vigorous offensive against the New Deal. Though it passed both houses, the bill was vetoed by President Roosevelt, and his veto was upheld.

Meanwhile, partly to blunt or head off this offensive, President Roosevelt took a most significant step in 1939 when he asked his Attorney General to appoint a committee on administrative procedure to make a thorough and comprehensive study of existing deficiencies and to point the way to improvements in the administrative process. The committee issued its report in 1941,[14] but the intervention of World War II delayed congressional action on its proposals. However, many of the committee's recommendations became part of the Federal Administrative Procedure Act of 1946, which, as amended, constitutes present federal law governing administrative procedure.[15]

The first major effort to improve administrative procedure on the state level began with the appointment, in 1937, of a committee on administrative tribunals of the American Bar Association. The committee confined its attention to the state level because another association committee—the Special Committee on Administrative Law —was studying federal administrative procedure at the time. The state committee issued a factual survey in 1938 and, in the following year, presented its recommendations, which were embodied in a bill to serve as a model for state legislation on the subject. The bill was considered for seven years by the National Conference of Commissioners on Uniform State Laws. The so-called Model State Administrative Procedure Act was finally approved by the Conference in 1946.

In the meantime, New York could claim the distinction of having a thorough study of its own procedures. In 1939, Governor Herbert Lehman appointed Robert M. Benjamin "to study, examine and investigate the exercise of quasi-judicial functions" by New York administrative agencies. Benjamin's report, submitted to the Governor

14 Committee on Administrative Procedure, *op. cit.*
15 60 U. S. Stat. 237 (1946).

in 1942, has served as a major source of information on state admin-istrative procedure.[16]

Important, although less well-known, studies have been made in other states. The California and Wisconsin studies are particularly noteworthy. Similar research has been conducted in Kentucky, Ohio, Virginia, and Minnesota.

Approximately half the states have enacted general administra-tive procedure legislation applying to one or more aspects of admin-istrative procedure.[17]

Wisconsin's experience illustrates the growing dilemma confront-ing state legislatures. The need for increased legislative control of administrative policy making was made more apparent to Wiscon-sin legislators when they returned to their homes after the 1951 legis-lative session. They were immediately besieged by constituents who complained of new "laws" that, upon inquiry, turned out to be new administrative policies or rules with the force and effect of law. The most controversial of the administrative rules was the so-called "milk house order" of the State Department of Agriculture. As part of a quality milk production program, it required producers of milk and cream to maintain a specially equipped milk house. Another ad-ministrative rule or policy, a provision of the State Board of Health's new "well code," required above-ground pump installations in well systems where water might be used for human consumption. Com-pliance with these policies imposed direct and substantial financial burdens upon many Wisconsin citizens.

The Wisconsin legislators responded intelligently when they met again in their 1953 session. They rejected such precipitous and ex-treme proposals as, for example, a bill to repeal all administrative rules and all authority to make them. Instead, the legislature directed the Wisconsin Legislative Council to conduct a comprehensive study of the rule-making process and to recommend remedial legislation. The council sought to frame a revision of its outdated administrative

16 Robert M. Benjamin, *Administrative Adjudication in the State of New York* (Albany: State of New York, 1942).
17 See Heady, *op. cit.*, and Harris, *op. cit.*

procedure act that would facilitate legislative control of rule making without unduly fettering administrative discretion. The effort was successful; the Wisconsin legislature enacted the revision in 1955.[18]

Few jurisdictions, unfortunately, have managed to frame remedial legislation that looks toward accommodation of increasing resort to administrative policy making with the ideals of representative and democratic government. As bureaucratization proceeds inexorably to coerce and to circumscribe individual behavior and group interests, a dilemma for democracy deepens in dimension.

[18] See Orrin L. Helstad and Earle Sachse, "A Study of Administrative Rule Making in Wisconsin," *Wisconsin Law Review* (1954), pp. 368-75, especially p. 369 at note 6; Wisconsin Legislative Council, *1955 Report, Administrative Rule Making*, pp. i-vi; Wisconsin Laws, Chapter 221 (1955); Orrin L. Helstad, "New Law on Administrative Rule Making," *Wisconsin Law Review* (May 1956), pp. 407-30; and Orrin L. Helstad and William W. Boyer, "Legislative Controls of Administrative Rule Making," *American Bar Association Journal*, XLI (November 1955), 1,048-51, especially p. 1,051.

PART ONE
✳✳✳
THE PROCESS
OF
POLICY MAKING

Chapter One

✻✻✻

The Policy-Making
Cycle

Legislatures are often baffled in their perennial attempts to control the administrative process because no two administrative agencies make policies in precisely the same manner. All the vicissitudes and vagaries of human behavior are reflected in the procedural heterogeneity of modern bureaucracy.

This sheer diversity has deterred social scientists from studying policy making in public administration in dimensions comprehensive enough to produce an identifiable process against which particular policy developments can be evaluated.[1] A conceptual framework for

[1] Though he stresses the policy and political responsibility of administrators, Paul Appleby has contributed a broad picture of "executive government" rather than an identifiable policy-making process in his *Policy and Administration* (University, Ala.: University of Alabama Press, 1949). See also his *Morality and Administration in Democratic Government,* Edward Douglass White Lectures on Citizenship (Baton Rouge: Louisiana State University and Agricultural and Mechanical College, 1952); Avery Leiserson, *Administrative Regulation: A Study in Representation of Interests* (Chicago: University of Chicago Press, 1942); E. Pendleton Herring, *Public Administration and the Public Interest* (New York: McGraw-Hill Book Co., Inc., 1936). For case studies of policy making, see Emmette S. Redford (ed.), *Public Administration and Policy Formation* (Austin, Tex.: University of Texas Press, 1956); Harold Stein (ed.), *Public Administration and Policy Development* (New York: Harcourt, Brace & Co., 1952). For administration of particular programs, see, for example: John M. Gaus and Leon O. Wolcott, *Public Adminis-*

descriptive analysis that transcends selected policies, procedures, agencies, and levels of government has yet to be constructed.

The broad descriptive analysis that follows is set forth to demonstrate the conception of five basic and sequential stages of agency policy making in public administration: (1) initiation; (2) preliminary drafting; (3) public participation; (4) final drafting; and (5) reviewing.[2]

INITIATION

The initiative for the development of agency policies ordinarily comes from any of three groups: legislative bodies; administrators; or private interest groups. Lesser sources can also be identified.

Legislative Bodies

Legislative bodies generally initiate administrative policy making in one of two ways: by a grant of authority directing or permitting an agency to adopt certain kinds of policies; or by passing legislation that supersedes or otherwise affects existing agency policies.

Grants of authority. Numerous statutes confer policy-making authority upon administrative agencies, but the number of such grants does not necessarily indicate the scope of an agency's authority to make policies. Some grants are very broad, as, for example, the delegation of authority to agencies to make reasonable policies for the protection of public health, or for the elimination of unfair trade

---

tration and the Department of Agriculture (Chicago: published for Committee on Public Administration of the Social Science Research Council by Public Administration Service, 1940); Emmette S. Redford, *Administration of National Economic Control* (New York: The Macmillan Company, 1952); Arthur W. Macmahon, John D. Millett, and Gladys Ogden, *The Administration of Federal Work Relief* (Chicago: published for the Committee on Public Administration of the Social Science Research Council by Public Administration Service, 1941); Philip Selznick, *TVA and the Grass Roots, A Study in the Sociology of Formal Organization* (Berkeley: University of California Press, 1949).

2 This conception of the basic process of agency policy making is drawn in part from the 1953-54 government-wide studies made by this writer, with Orrin L. Helstad, of policy making in seventy-one Wisconsin state agencies, as discussed in the Preface to this study.

practices or unfair labor practices. Other grants of authority may be relatively narrow, such as a statutory directive that an agency make policies to prevent, eradicate, and control communicable diseases of honeybees. There are even narrower grants—that an agency prescribe a definition of "epilepsy," for example. Some statutes direct agencies to make policies, whereas others merely grant them authority to do so. Sometimes, no reference of any kind is made to agency policy making in the enabling legislation, when obviously the agency could not accomplish its purposes without formulating and applying policies.[3] However broad the legislature's language of delegation may be, not all administrators can always know whether the legislature requires or permits that certain kinds of policies be formulated and adopted by the agency.

Superseding policies. Though an agency has adopted policies to implement legislation, subsequently the legislature itself may adopt standards that supersede or otherwise cause their modification. Of course, if an agency fails to recast its policies to correspond with legislative change, it risks their invalidation by the courts.

Administrators

Agency personnel. It is elementary that those closest to the everyday problems of an agency will prove a productive source of ideas as to the way in which its policy-making discretion ought to be exercised. Indeed, personnel of administrative agencies constitute the primary source of rules that take the form of interpretations and statements of agency enforcement or licensing policies. Moreover, problems identified in the application of existing agency policies may cause policy revisions. For example, fish management personnel in many states observe the movement of fish species from one area to another, observe seasonal concentrations of fish and spawning grounds, and

---

[3] Courts have held that agencies granted licensing powers have implied authority to make rules; see, for example, Whitney v. Watson, 85 N. H. 238, 157 A. 78 (1931). Indeed, one court went so far as almost to insist that an agency adopt rules to guide decisions related to licensing in the absence of legislation directing the agency to adopt rules (Heitmeyer v. Federal Communications Commission, 68 App. D. C. 95 F. 2d 91 [1937]).

thereby determine in certain instances that fish refuges should be established to protect and replenish stock. Policies governing seasons for the hunting of various species of game are initiated in a similar way.

Some agencies actually formalize procedures for internal policy initiation by prescribing appropriate forms to be completed by agency personnel for such purposes, or by fixing upon designated employees the responsibility of recommending policies regularly.

Intergovernmental relations. The actions of administrators of one governmental jurisdiction may cause or influence corresponding policy adjustments in other jurisdictions.

The impact of federal government action on policy making by state agencies is now clearly recognized.[4] States that wish to have their agricultural products marketed beyond their own boundaries at highest prices, for example, should adopt and enforce relevant federal grading standards.

Federal action also vitally affects administrative policy making in local governments, especially in the 168 metropolitan areas in which most of the nation's population is located.[5] Thus, local planning commissions must abide by federal standards in order to receive federal funds for urban renewal and redevelopment projects.

Not only does the federal government require state and local agencies to formulate and apply certain policies, on pain of withholding federal grants-in-aid, but it indirectly influences policy making by state and local agencies. Interdependence of the various levels is growing constantly, to the extent that almost every new federal program causes policy responses within state and local bureaucracies.

It is not uncommon, moreover, for administrators of one jurisdiction to rely on the experience of other jurisdictions as a source of

4 See the following studies of the Commission on Intergovernmental Relations (Washington, D. C.: U. S. Gov't. Printing Office, 1955): *A Survey Report on the Impact of Federal Grants-in-aid on the Structure and Functions of State and Local Governments*; *A Description of Twenty-five Federal Grant-in-aid Programs*; *A Report to the President for Transmittal to the Congress.* See also Selznick, *op. cit.*

5 Commission on Intergovernmental Relations, *An Advisory Committee Report on Local Government* (Washington, D. C.: U. S. Gov't. Printing Office, 1955), pp. 24-26.

administrative policies. For example, the secretaries of the state boards of pharmacy of Minnesota, New Jersey, and Wisconsin have frequently corresponded about matters of mutual concern. But the sharing of administrative experience is most significant for policy making when administrators pool their efforts within the framework of national associations.

National associations. National associations of administrators draw their membership from the various states and, sometimes, from the federal government. They meet annually, study common problems through committees, and make recommendations to promote efficiency and uniformity and to elevate standards of regulation and general policy. The national associations often foster regional organizations of the same type and with similar functions. The deliberations and actions of these organizations are of great importance as sources of administrative policies. More than other types of organizations, they represent the opinions and interests of public administrators in their respective fields.

Illustrative of nationwide associations of public officers is the American Association of Motor Vehicle Administrators, which exerts significant influence as a source of policies of the motor vehicle departments of the states represented. This association seeks to advance uniformity of reciprocity agreements entered into by various states and to improve policies concerning motor vehicle registration, driver-examination procedure, licensing, law enforcement, and highway safety.

Equally effective as a source of administrative policies is the National Association of Securities Administrators. Securities administrators of some eighteen states implemented, by prior agreement, certain 1953 "directives" formulated by the association's committee on investment companies. Besides attempting to influence the adoption of investment regulations, the association promotes uniformity of legislation, forms, and licensing requirements for dealers and brokers in securities. At least forty states have adopted its uniform application form for registration of securities.

Intragovernmental associations. In addition to nationwide organizations of government officials, associations within the same governmental jurisdiction have been formed to pursue purposes and exert influence of a nature similar to that of national associations in the formulation of administrative policies.

In the federal government, two organizations have been outstanding in this respect—the Federal Business Association and the Federal Personnel Council, the former comprising agency directors having the general purpose of promoting discussions of policy matters of mutual concern, and the latter comprising both agency directors and personnel directors. The express purpose of the Federal Personnel Council is "to promote through study and discussion the application, interpretation, and development of personnel policies and practices . . . throughout the Federal service."[6]

Statewide associations have been formed by certain local government officers and employees to influence state policy making. They range from associations that serve in advisory capacities to state administrative departments to those which act as intragovernmental pressure groups. Familiar among such groups are organizations of policemen, firemen, recreation leaders, and public education personnel. Each group may be divided into several organizations. Typically, public education personnel in a state may form state-wide associations for each of several subgroups—county superintendents, school boards, school administrators, vocational school directors, and teachers, to mention only a few. The recommendations of these organizations concerning teacher certification and other important policies are often actively sought by the appropriate state agency.

Another type of intragovernmental association is the public employees' union. Although generally denied the right to strike, public employees may bargain, petition, and otherwise exert policy influence through their own associations.

Private Interest Groups

Pressure group influence in public policy making is not restricted to the familiar practice of lobbying among the nation's legislators.

6 W. Brooke Graves, *Public Administration in a Democratic Society* (Boston: D. C. Heath & Co., 1950), p. 253.

Much administrative policy making is initiated by private interest groups.

Complaints or recommendations from regulated industries, or from other affected interests, provide the most important single source of policies adopted by some agencies.

Wisconsin's experience. The impact of private pressure upon administrative policy making is perhaps best illustrated by reference to the experience of one governmental jurisdiction in which a pertinent study has been made—the state government of Wisconsin.[7]

In Wisconsin's Department of Agriculture, complaints of agricultural interests account for more than 50 per cent of the department's rule-making proceedings. For example, in 1946 the members of Wisconsin's brick cheese industry succeeded in having the department change the holding period for brick cheese.

Ordinarily, the changes sought by private interests are narrow, but sometimes they are far-reaching and significant. Thus, proposals of the powerful Wisconsin Dairy Federation were the source of the agriculture department's code of regulations prescribing minimum standards for sanitary milk production in "America's Dairyland."

Numerous other examples of policy initiation by Wisconsin interest groups can be cited. A petition by the Wisconsin Motor Carriers Association resulted in a Public Service Commission policy that, in effect, amended the certificates of all "common carriers for property" so that authority to serve Milwaukee would include authority to serve an A. O. Smith plant located one and one-half miles outside the city. The original Industrial Commission policies of 1917, which regulated the hours of labor for women, were initiated by joint petition of the Wisconsin Federation of Labor, the Milwaukee Council of Social Agencies, and the Wisconsin Consumers League. More recent changes in the Industrial Commission's building code provisions, which relate to the summer occupancy of industrial camps, were initiated by the Wisconsin Canners Association, whose members are dependent on migrant labor. Rating organizations and insurance

[7] Wisconsin Legislative Council, *1955 Report, Administrative Rule Making*, pp. 29-31.

companies have long exerted considerable influence upon policy making by Wisconsin's Insurance Department. The Wisconsin Savings and Loan League has been known on occasion to obtain adoption of its proposals by the state savings and loan department *immediately* upon their presentation.

Not all complaints or petitions, of course, result in new policies or in the repeal of old policies. Thus, the Public Service Commission denied a petition of the Wisconsin State Telephone Association (representing 90 per cent of the state's telephone industry) to establish telephone exchange boundaries for the state. The commission reasoned that such a policy would be of doubtful legality and that, in any case, it would involve the assumption of an undue administrative burden.

The following is a list of only some of the many trade and professional organizations that have exerted significant influence on regulations of the state regulatory and licensing agencies in Wisconsin:

American Institute of Accountants
Wisconsin Society of Certified Public Accountants
Wisconsin Association of Watchmakers
Wisconsin Retail Jewelers Association
American Medical Association
Wisconsin Chiropractic Association
Wisconsin State Dental Society
Wisconsin Optometric Association
American Optometric Association
American Pharmaceutical Association
Wisconsin Pharmaceutical Association
United Druggists Association
Hospital Pharmacists Society
National Association of Retail Druggists
National Boxing Association
American Institute of Architects
Wisconsin Bar Association
Wisconsin Association of Real Estate Brokers
Public School Retirement Association
State College Retirement Association

University Retirement Association
National Retired Teachers' Association
Sulphite Pulp Manufacturers' Research League
Society of Automotive Engineers
Wisconsin Automotive Trades Association
Used Car Dealers Association
Wisconsin Finance Association
Wisconsin Bankers Association
Wisconsin Credit Union League
Wisconsin Association of Small Loan Companies
Wisconsin Well Drillers, Inc.
Wisconsin Farm Bureau Federation
Wisconsin Dairy Federation
Wisconsin Creamery Association
Wisconsin State Beekeepers Association

Incorporation of private standards.   Typically, a professional organization whose members are licensed by the state will formulate standards of ethics and professional conduct and will have them given the force of law by securing their adoption by the state licensing agency as administrative rules or regulations. Agencies do this either by incorporating such standards directly into their rules or by incorporating them by reference. Wisconsin's Board of Accountancy has followed the former method. Its code of ethics and regulations governing C.P.A. examinations is based primarily on the code of ethics and examination standards formulated by the American Institute of Accountants and approved by the Wisconsin Society of Certified Public Accountants.

Agency incorporation of the policies of professional organizations by reference constitutes the most extreme form of influence by interest groups on administrative policy making. For example, by mere reference in its rules, Wisconsin's Board of Examiners in Optometry incorporated the code of ethics of the American Optometric Association. On March 4, 1948, the board defined unprofessional conduct as "including any conduct contrary to the code of ethics of the American Optometric Association," reference being to the association's sixteen-page *Optometric Code of Ethics and Supplements* (1947).

The American Optometric Association is a private professional organization and has no governmental or lawmaking responsibility to act in the interests of Wisconsin's citizenry. Yet the board, by this single action, announced that in Wisconsin the association's code of ethics has the force of law as it exists and as it may be amended in the future—not by the board, but by the association.[8]

The familiar administrative practice of incorporation by reference is tantamount to declaring that some organization outside and independent of government shall determine, currently and in the future, the substance of those governmental regulations which affect the members of that organization.[9]

Lesser Sources

Private individuals, legal departments, courts, and advisory committees, though of less importance than other initiators of administrative policy making, on occasion may motivate administrators to make new policy or to change existing policy.

Private individuals. Infrequently, an individual acting alone may evoke a policy response from a government agency. This is what happened, for example, when the assistant general manager of the Equity Co-operative Live Stock Association in Milwaukee wrote a letter, dated July 28, 1947, to the director of Wisconsin's Department of Agriculture requesting that western North Dakota be included as "range" territory "so as to make it possible to ship in heifers up to

[8] Wisconsin Legislative Council, *Interim Report II on Administrative Rule Making* (Madison, Wisc.: State Capitol, 1954), pp. 360-61. For general discussion of the great influence exercised over policy and administration in government by "private associations," see, for example, Grant McConnell, "The Spirit of Private Government," *American Political Science Review*, LII (September 1958), 754-70; and J. A. C. Grant, "The Guild Returns to America, I and II" *Journal of Politics*, IV (August 1942), 303-36, 458-77.

[9] For similar practices in jurisdictions other than Wisconsin, see Walter Gellhorn, *Administrative Law, Cases and Comments* (Brooklyn: Foundation Press, 1947), pp. 88-89.

two years of age from that area without having a bangs test on them before they are loaded. . . . As I am making a buying trip west the first week of September I am wondering if a hearing could be held before that time and have the regulation amended." A public hearing was held on August 11, with only two members of the public present. On August 14, just seventeen days after the request was made and two weeks prior to the buying trip, the requested amendment was issued.[10] Successful policy initiatives by private individuals, however, are exceptions, compared with organizational influences.

Legal departments. City law departments, state attorneys general, or the federal Department of Justice occasionally advise an agency to adopt or change certain policies. Central legal departments are most important when agencies, such as professional licensing boards, lack attorneys but require legal advice concerning proposed policies.

Courts. Though court decisions rarely cause administrative policy changes, few agencies are free from judicial review of their exercise of policy-making discretion. Occasionally, therefore, courts decide that agencies have made policies beyond the authority conferred on them. But court influence on agency policy making may have far greater significance than the number of pertinent court decisions implies. The Wisconsin study found that agencies usually modify policies of doubtful legality rather than risk adverse court decisions.

Advisory committees. Advisory committees—discussed more fully subsequently—generally review policy proposals that have already been formulated. Sometimes, however, they actually initiate the policy-making process, in spite of one observer's warning that "public advisory boards cannot and should not initiate policy. . . ."[11]

It is apparent that most administrative policies are initiated by variable and informal precedures, such as direct contact with agency personnel through letter, telephone, or personal conversation. It is

[10] Wisconsin Legislative Council, *1955 Report, Administrative Rule Making,* pp. 31-32.
[11] David S. Brown, "The Public Advisory Board as an Instrument of Government," *Public Administration Review,* XV (Summer 1955), 196-204, at p. 198. See Wisconsin Legislative Council, *1955 Report, Administrative Rule Making,* p. 33.

also clear that a division or agency head usually acquires his ideas about agency policies from others. Policy ideas generally do not spring from his own contemplation.

PRELIMINARY DRAFTING

Policy conception is coincident with making the original draft of the proposal. But seldom does preliminary drafting consist merely of a simple and discrete act. This stage may involve several drafts before agency authorities are satisfied that a policy idea has crystallized into a proposed agency policy. The first draft may be made by any interested person within or outside an administrative agency. Practice varies considerably. Generally, however, the original draft of a policy proposal is prepared by the person on the agency staff who is most familiar with the subject dealt with in the proposal.

Normally, the author of the draft submits it to his administrative superior (who may be a division head or the actual head, or heads, of the agency, depending on the nature of the organization). The latter may then take a number of actions. Sometimes he will ask other members of the agency's staff for suggestions. He may submit the draft to industry representatives or associations, or conduct informal conferences with others who are likely to be affected by the policy if it is adopted. The draft may be referred to a special or statutory advisory committee—often an important step in the policy formulation process—or to the legal department of the government jurisdiction.

Where the drafting process is relatively unstructured or informal, as it usually is, the number of people involved normally varies according to the size of the organization. In a large organization, the formulation of policy proposals is a staff-wide process. This is not to say that every principal staff member of the respective first- or second-line component of the organization's hierarchy customarily participates in the drafting of each proposal. Rather, the participants vary according to the substance or character of the proposal. For example, in one agency division, a policy proposal may initially be drafted by the division's director in collaboration with the assistant director. If the division has no legal counsel on its staff, the director may rely upon his government's legal department for advice in drafting the proposal, or, if they are available, upon attorneys elsewhere within his parent organization. He may also solicit suggestions from field personnel.

In another division of the same parent organization, the director may solicit relevant information and assistance from any or all of the following, depending upon the nature of the particular proposal: field personnel; public and private agencies throughout the nation; other government agencies of the same jurisdiction; university experts; and lay persons who may or may not comprise affected agency clientele. Some few policy proposals may even be drafted by the head of the large organization with or without the participation of his principal deputies.

If no regular procedure is established for policy formulation in a large organization, the drafting process will be conditioned by the variable factors of the proposal's substance, the behavior of the mixed organization, and the behavior of the individuals involved.

PUBLIC PARTICIPATION

After the preliminary draft has been made, and depending upon the circumstances, agency administrators may choose to elicit the advice of representatives of the public, especially of those who are among the agency's clientele and are likely to be affected by the policy.

There are three principal methods by which an administrator may induce public participation in agency policy making. He may use (1) informal conferences and consultations; (2) advisory committees; and (3) public hearings.

Informal Conferences

The use of conferences is the simplest and most informal method of achieving interest-group or public participation in policy making.[12] The administrator may choose to discuss proposed policies with affected persons orally or in writing, by prearranged meeting or fortuitous contact, singly or in groups.

However such contacts are made, the practice of holding informal conferences with parties interested in proposed policies appears to be followed at one time or another by almost all administrative agencies. Large administrative establishments use the conference technique more extensively than smaller agencies. The more controversial the policy proposal, moreover, the more disposed are many administrators to resort to conferences. The technique affords the administrator an opportunity to (1) identify onerous provisions, (2) forecast administrative difficulties, and (3) engineer the consent of affected interests.

The specific procedures employed by an administrator in conferences are situational in character, varying considerably from agency to agency and from case to case. Some conferences are held prior to drafting and are oriented toward problem identification in relation to policy initiation. Others are held after the tentative policy draft is made and are oriented toward review of the policy proposal. Still others are used in conjunction with, or as supplements to, other participation techniques—advisory committees and public hearings, for example—that an administrator may employ. In these instances, the conferences usually precede resort to advisory committee meetings or public hearings.

Some jurisdictions hire members of the public as part-time consultants, on either an *ad hoc* or a continuing basis, to advise on agency policy making.[13] This technique involves a relationship between

12 Little systematic research has been done concerning the use of conferences or consultations in the administrative process, despite their widespread acceptance. Martin Kriesberg and Harold Guetzkow, "The Use of Conferences in the Administrative Process," *Public Administration Review*, X (Spring 1950), 93-98, at p. 93.

13 Many consultants are drawn from universities. For example, seventeen members of the faculty of Harvard's Graduate School of Public Administration served as consultants during 1960 to federal agencies, six were active in state and local administration, three functioned with foreign governments, and twelve were consultants to various research institutions serving the armed services under contract (Don K. Price, "Preparing for the Highest Levels of Government Service," *Harvard Today* [Spring 1961], p. 14). Government also appears increasingly disposed, since World War II, to retain private consulting firms to study and recommend im-

members of the public and the government agency that is clearly distinguishable from the informal conference or consultation. For one thing, it is a more formal and regular relationship. In addition, there is some question whether the individual concerned remains a member of the public as distinguished from an agency employee when, in fact, he is compensated for services rendered to the agency.

Advisory Committees

The administrative practices of consulting or conferring with private interests leads easily to the establishment of advisory committees comprised of such interests.

So many kinds of boards, commissions, and committees are now being used for public policy making that distinctions must be drawn. This discussion is concerned with advisory committees at the agency level that have been created to advise administrators on how to exercise their policy-making discretion. It is not concerned with special commissions created by chief executives or legislatures to make comprehensive studies of major government problem areas and recommend remedial legislation.[14]

Presidential commissions, and similarly established state and mu-

---

provements in the administrative process, usually to increase efficiency and reduce operating costs. These studies indirectly affect agency policy making. Thus, the Public Administration Service has conducted such studies of the insular government of the Virgin Islands and of position classification in Pennsylvania's Commonwealth government. The ten-volume study of the U. S. Veterans Administration by the firm of Booz, Allen, and Hamilton, Management Consultants, was the basis for a sweeping reorganization of that agency. The Pennsylvania Economy League has conducted studies ranging from the collection and disposal of garbage in Pennsylvania's Allegheny County to reorganization of the Governor's Office of that state.

14 Theodore Roosevelt was the first president to use this latter device extensively. Herbert Hoover established some sixty-two commissions during the first sixteen months of his administration. More than one hundred commissions are reported to have been created during the first eight years of Franklin Roosevelt's presidency, whereas only twenty major commissions were created during Harry Truman's tenure. The first four and one-half years of the Eisenhower Administration witnessed the establishment of eleven such groups (Alan L. Dean, "Advantages and Disadvantages in the Use of *Ad Hoc* Commissions for Policy Formulation," a paper prepared for presentation at the Annual Meeting of the American Political Science Association, New York, September 5-7, 1957, multilithed, pp. 2-3). Illustrative of

nicipal *ad hoc* commissions, play an increasingly important role in modern American government. However, they do not *directly* influence the exercise of policy discretion by the administrator at the agency level. This is the role of agency advisory committees, among others. Reports of top-level *ad hoc* commissions are directed more toward the formulation of parent legislation and executive orders than toward that of administrative rules and regulations and other subordinate agency policies.

Extent of Use. Practically every type of advisory committee can be found in public administration. These committees vary as to manner of appointment of members, regularity and frequency of meetings, and formality of proceedings. They are in common use throughout the nation at every level of government—national, state, and local—and at various administrative levels. They have multiplied as rapidly as government functions have increased and broadened.

Before 1938 there were fewer than one hundred advisory committees in the entire federal government. By 1955 the Department of Agriculture alone had fifty advisory committees at the national level, and the number for the federal service as a whole was reported to be several hundred.[15] Even this latter estimate of rapid growth was undoubtedly understated. Responses to a 1957 questionnaire indicated that some five thousand committees advised various agencies of the federal government.[16]

Municipalities create advisory committees on subjects ranging

---

such commissions during the Eisenhower Administration were the second Commission on Organization of the Executive Branch of the Government (Hoover Commission), the Commission on Intergovernmental Relations (Kestnbaum Commission), the President's Commission on Veterans' Pensions (Bradley Commission), and the Commission on Foreign Economic Policy (Randall Commission) (*ibid.,* p. 3). See also Carl Marcy, *Presidential Commissions* (New York: King's Crown Press, 1945); Fritz Morstein-Marx, "Temporary Presidential Advisory Commissions" (unpublished staff paper, U. S. Bureau of the Budget, 1952).

15 Brown, *op. cit. supra,* note 11. See also Lewis C. Mainzer, "Science Democratized: Advisory Committees on Research," *Public Administration Review,* XVIII (Autumn 1958), 314-23.

16 U. S. Congress, House of Representatives, Committee on Government Operations, Second Report, *Availability of Information from Federal Departments and Agencies,* H. R. Report No. 157, 85th Cong., 1st sess., February 22, 1957, p. 39.

from community planning and slum clearance to mass transit and smoke control. State governments have committees on education, agriculture, and a myriad of other state concerns. The federal government uses advisory committees on subjects as varied as automatic data processing, cotton export, and shoelaces for members of the armed forces.

According to John M. Gaus, the practice of using advisory committees and other public participation devices is so widespread that new conceptions of the nature of the modern state need to be formulated. Expressing his belief in the essential value of these "devices of participation," Professor Gaus has called attention to the "need for a theory of public administration that will reflect them."[17]

In 1911 Wisconsin's State Industrial Commission became the first government agency in the United States to establish an advisory committee. A study of forty-six Wisconsin state agencies reveals that ten agencies make extensive use of advisory committees. Some of them are prescribed by statute. Agency discretion accounts for the existence of other continuing, if not permanent, committees. In addition, numerous temporary advisory committees have been created from time to time.[18]

The employment by state regulatory agencies of advisory code-formulating committees, composed of representatives of employers, employees, and agency staff, has been particularly marked in Wisconsin, where the ideas of John R. Commons have been especially influential.[19]

Types of committees. In terms of composition and function, three types of advisory committees may be discerned. The technical advisory committee is composed primarily of experts, and its purpose is to provide technical or scientific advice to the agency rather than to

17 John M. Gaus, "Public Participation in Federal Programs," in O. B. Conaway, Jr. (ed.), *Democracy in Federal Administration* (Washington, D. C.: U. S. Department of Agriculture Graduate School, 1956), pp. 7, 16.

18 Wisconsin Legislative Council, *1955 Report, Administrative Rule Making*, p. 39, and Part I of Appendix II-A.

19 John R. Commons, *Myself* (New York: The Macmillan Company, 1934), pp. 154-59.

represent interests. The interdepartmental coordinating committee is composed of government officials whose function is to give advice on problem areas that cut across agency lines.[20] Finally, there is the representative advisory committee, whose members represent interest groups or the general public in advising agencies on policy formulation.

These three types of committees are not mutually exclusive. Sometimes they may profitably be combined. An advisory committee of one board of health, for example, has elements of all three types; its membership includes technical experts from medicine, nursing, and architecture, a public officer of the welfare department, and representatives of the general public, labor, agriculture, and a hospital association.

Representative committees.   Representative advisory committees contribute most to administrative policy making; therefore, they are the primary concern of this discussion.

No two of these committees are alike in every respect. Like the informal conference or consultation, they are situational in character. Some committees are required to exist by statutes that may or may not specify interests to be represented. Others are created on an agency's own initiative, either with or without express statutory authority. Some exist to advise on specific rule making only. The purpose of others is to aid in the formulation of complete code revisions or to advise on general agency policy making. Some committees are permanent, while others are only temporary. Some are rather large, while others are small.

Membership on some committees is determined wholly by the agency to be advised. But often an agency authorizes interest groups to nominate or select their own representatives. Occasionally, committee membership is determined either in whole or in part by the chief executive of the jurisdiction in which the agency concerned is located.

Committees differ also with respect to compensation and operating

[20] See, for example, Harold Guetzkow, "Interagency Committee Usage," *Public Administration Review*, X (Summer 1950), 190-96.

procedures. Some committees are compensated on a per diem basis; others receive only expenses, and many receive no compensation. Some committees meet regularly and frequently; others seldom meet. Some keep a complete transcript or other record of their proceedings, whereas many committees fail even to keep minutes.

However, assuming that an appropriate advisory committee exists and that the administrator decides to consult it on a proposed policy, three general methods appear available to him. He can ask the committee to review the proposal at its regular meeting, if one is held periodically. He can call the committee to meet in special session to consider the proposed policy. Or he can consult with committee members individually or in combinations.

Among the advantages that representative advisory committees, as well as conferences, afford an administrator is that their use makes available to him information, advice, and opinions from representatives of affected interests. These techniques are therefore implemented to aid him in making informed policy decisions. At the same time, those consulted have the assurance that they have been heard.

Public Hearings

Public hearings differ from conferences and advisory committees in that hearings are publicly announced in advance and *any* interested person is permitted to attend and testify.[21] Advance public notice and accessibility to the general public are usually considered to be the primary requisites of a public hearing. Apart from these characteristics, the practices and procedures at public hearings vary greatly.

Required hearings. Often a government agency has no choice but to hold a public hearing prior to adoption of a policy proposal because the legislature has stipulated that a hearing be held, in spite of the fact that the legislature has otherwise delegated considerable policy-making authority to the agency. Many congressional enactments, state statutes, and municipal ordinances—as well as general

21 Committee on Administrative Procedure, *Final Report of the Attorney General's Committee on Administrative Procedure*, p. 105.

administrative procedure acts—require that hearings be held prior to promulgation of certain categories of rules or regulations.

When a statute requires a public hearing, however, it rarely prescribes what kind of hearing must be held. The result is that no two agencies conduct policy-making hearings in precisely the same manner, and even within the same agency practices and procedures may vary from hearing to hearing and among agency divisions.

Types of hearings. Nevertheless, two types of public hearings are broadly distinguishable—formal and informal. When the hearing appears akin to a courtroom proceeding, it may be classified as formal. Such hearings, though differing in the degree of their formality, are characterized by one or more of these features: testimony under oath; transcription of proceedings; cross-examination; exhibits; counsel; briefs; rules of evidence; and other aspects of judicial procedure. When the hearing resembles the usual town hall type of meeting, then it is decidedly informal. The more controversial a policy proposal is likely to be, the more disposed is an administrator to formalize the hearing. In few instances, however, are the procedures sufficiently formal, uniform, and inflexible to permit a relatively generic description.

FINAL DRAFTING

When no public hearings are held and no other public participation devices are invoked, the drafting of the final policy is not a distinguishable step in the policy-making process. If public participation is elicited, however, it is generally followed by a period of deliberation and revision with reference to the information obtained or views expressed at the participation stage. Thereby, the basic objectives of securing the advice of the public are realized. Once the draft has been completed to the satisfaction of agency personnel, it is submitted to that body or person vested by law with the authority to adopt the proposal as a policy having the force of law.

It is not unusual for the legislature to require that an agency's policy be approved by some outside authority, such as the jurisdiction's legal officer, chief executive, department of administrative procedure, if any, or a legislative review body. In the absence of any statutory clearance requirements, the policy-making process is completed upon the central filing of the policy, if required, and its official publication as may be prescribed by law. Its implementation awaits only the policy's effective date.

REVIEWING

Agency policy making is a never-ending process. It involves modifying existing policies as well as adopting new ones. Policy enforcement frequently poses greater difficulties than policy formulation. Evaluation of the workability and fairness of existing policies is, therefore, a normal, if not explicitly conscious, stage in the making of policy decisions.

No policy is eternal, but whether an agency will modify a policy upon request depends upon a limitless variety of factors. There are two important considerations in this respect: The more controversial an existing agency policy is, the more likely it is to be changed; and the more extensive public participation in the policy's formulation is, the less difficult its enforcement after adoption will be and, hence, the less likely it is to be readily changed.

CONCLUSION

Once administrative review of an existing policy is initiated, the policy-making process may be regarded as commencing again.

Thus, agency policy making may be considered a cyclical process with five sequential stages: initiation; preliminary drafting; public participation; final drafting; and reviewing. Though the process frequently occurs in a shortened form, with the skipping or merging of stages, broadly conceived it involves a logical sequence of development from one stage to another. Reviewing makes the process cyclical because this stage brings the sequence back to substantially the point at which it began. The policy-making cycle may be graphically represented by the diagram below.

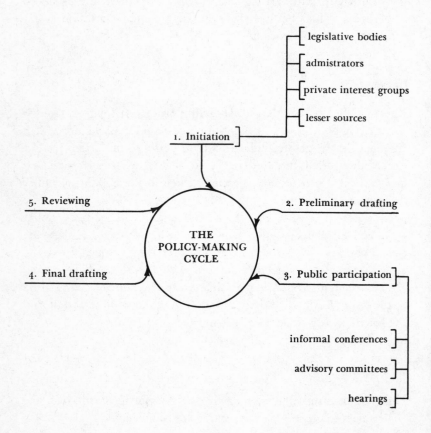

Chapter Two

✳✳✳

The Politics of
Initiation

To describe the policy-making cycle is not to identify and probe its central problems. Accordingly, this chapter and the next discuss problems of the first and third stages of the cycle—initiation and public participation. These stages involve interaction of public administration with its environment or ecology.

The discussion of initiation in the last chapter discerns principal and lesser sources of policy ideas. Turning now to the first stage of the policy-making cycle—initiation—we seek here to isolate problems facing administrators at critical moments of decision whether to reject ideas or to proceed with them as policy proposals worthy of consideration for possible adoption. These moments of decision emerge during the policy initiation stage. Proper analysis of policy initiation not only includes identification of sources of policy ideas—as already discussed—but also the various problems and pressures that influence policy-initiating decisions of administrators. In other words, meaningful discussion of the crystallization of policy ideas merits analysis of the *politics* of initiation.

THE LEGISLATURE

The administrator has discretion to exercise, delegated by parent authority of either the legislature or a superior executive. Regarding the legislature, he must interpret the language in which it has couched its collective will, for usually it is the legislature that has created his organization, has vested it with its administrative powers, and has financially determined the scope of its work. But this is not the only problem that the administrator must consider with respect to the legislature. He may be required intermittently to appear before committees of the legislature to impart information and to assess legislative interest concerning agency policy problems. In addition, individual legislators, often acting in behalf of constituent interests, may attempt to initiate or obstruct agency policy proposals. From the legislature alone, then, the administrator faces problems, among others, of statutory interpretation, committee investigations, and pressures from individual legislators.

Statutory Interpretation

One factor conditioning an administrator's decision whether to proceed with a policy idea as an agency proposal is his interpretation of whether a statute *requires* or *permits* his agency to adopt certain policies.

Many statutory authorizations are stated in terms of "may" or "shall." Not all administrators similarly interpret these terms. In Wisconsin, for example, some agencies have adopted rules on subjects whenever they were referred to in statutes, no matter whether the statutes were drafted in permissive or in mandatory language. Other agencies have failed to adopt policies even when governing statutes seemingly directed them to do so by mandatory admonitions of the term "shall." The reasons given for the latter practice varied, but generally the administrator asserted either that the statute itself was complete or detailed enough, or that he preferred to apply the statute directly by proceeding on a case-by-case adjudicatory basis, that is, by issuing special orders rather than rules. In no instance did an administrator admit negligence.[1]

In addition, only twelve of forty-six Wisconsin state agencies com-

[1] Wisconsin Legislative Council, *1955 Report, Administrative Rule Making*, pp. 24-25.

plied with the mandatory directive of the state's general administrative procedure act to adopt rules of agency procedure relating to
petitions for rules, presumably because formal petitions to adopt
rules were seldom made to agencies. In one instance, the wording of
an agency rule remained unchanged even after the statutory authority for the rule's existence had been repealed by the legislature. The
administrator responsible admitted negligence as the reason, for no
other explanation was available for him in such a situation.[2]

A legislature can generally effect administrative policy changes by
statutory action that is inconsistent with existing agency policies. But
merely by use of mandatory language in statutory directives or requirements—by use of "shall" rather than "may"—legislatures cannot
be assured that commensurate agency policy will be initiated. Reasons
that are sufficient to an administrator may condition his choice not
to initiate certain policies even when, seemingly, he is required by
statute to initiate them. He should be aware that in such instances he
risks the hostility of the legislature.

Legislative Committees

Most work of Congress, and of state and city legislatures, is done in
committees. The impact of legislative committees on administrative
action is increasingly recognized.[3] A legislative body as a whole can

---

[2] Rather than formulate policy proposals and publish them as rules within his delegated authority, one state insurance commissioner preferred to persuade
the legislature to enact into statutes the policies he favored. This method had two
unfortunate results: overly detailed and voluminous statutes on insurance; and the
disposition of the insurance commissioner to make and enforce agency policies
without publishing them as required (*ibid.*).

[3] See, for example, the pertinent portions of J. Leiper Freeman, *The Political
Process: Executive Bureau-Legislative Committee Relations* (Garden City: Double-
day & Company, 1955); Bertram M. Gross, *The Legislative Struggle* (New York:
McGraw-Hill Book Co., Inc., 1953); Earl Latham, *The Group Basis of Politics*
(Ithaca: Published for Amherst College by Cornell University Press, 1952); V. O.
Key, Jr., *Politics, Parties, and Pressure Groups* (3rd ed.; New York: Thomas Y.
Crowell Company, 1952); David B. Truman, *The Governmental Process* (New York:
Alfred A. Knopf, Inc., 1951); Charles S. Hyneman, *Bureaucracy in a Democracy*
(New York: Harper & Brothers, 1950); O. B. Conaway, Jr. (ed.), *Legislative-
Executive Relationships* (Washington, D. C.: U. S. Department of Agriculture
Graduate School, 1953).

dispose of the more important policy issues by enacting statutes. But to understand legislative-administrative relations it is also necessary to focus on the behavior of committees and their individual members, as well as on the constituent and interest pressures behind them. The actual pattern of these relations is incredibly complex. Committee obstruction of agency policy making and review of existing policy are more apparent and less subtle than initiation of specific agency rules or regulations.[4] Moreover, general program and policy, on the one hand, and specific decisions in adjudicatory cases, on the other hand, capture legislative attention more than do particular agency policy choices.[5] Nevertheless, the impact of legislative scrutiny upon administrative decision making, and hence on policy initiation, is profound. What matters here is not that an administrator is forced by a vote or an overt instruction of a legislative committee to initiate a particular policy, for seldom does this happen. More important is an administrator's assessment of the given ecology within which he must make his policy decisions. For efficacious policy initiation, he must attempt to perceive and anticipate the behavior of legislative committees and the environment reflected by them.

In addition to the relation of appropriations committees and their subcommittees to day-to-day administrative activity, standing committees often hold hearings—some extending over months or even years—that dig deeply into the administrative process. Administrators are sometimes made virtual defendants in these proceedings. "When any sector of the administrative branch is under searching investigation by either standing or select committee, it may be told in detail and emphatically what it is required to do under provisions of the law and what it ought to do in the exercise of its discretion."[6] For example, with respect to the Office of Price Administration in the

4 V. O. Key, Jr., "Legislative Control," in Fritz Morstein-Marx (ed.), *Elements of Public Administration* (2nd ed.; Englewood Cliffs, N. J.: Prentice-Hall, Inc., 1959), pp. 312-33, especially pp. 316, 317.

5 See, for example, Seymour Scher, "Congressional Committee Members as Independent Agency Overseers: A Case Study," *American Political Science Review*, LIV (December 1960), 911-20. Scher discusses congressional intervention in adjudicatory decisions before the National Labor Relations Board.

6 Hyneman, *op. cit.*, p. 166.

1946 hearings on the price control controversy, the U.S. Senate Committee on Banking and Currency "constituted itself a kind of superadministrative agency, intervening capriciously and depending upon business to initiate the process. [Senator Homer] Capehart got an assurance that a price increase would be granted the cheese industry, and [Senator Robert A.] Taft a promise of immediate action on evaporated milk."[7]

Even a threat of committee action may initiate policy. When staff members of legislative committees make inquiries, administrators may respond by making educated guesses about future committee behavior and by adjusting their policies accordingly. Legislative committees "are always ready to summon an executive officer to justify a decision he has made, and the ever-present possibility is as likely to influence his actions as the actual summons. Approval by the key members of such committees may be sought before taking discretionary action of various kinds."[8]

The investigative function of the legislature, exercised through its committees, has probably received more attention and created more controversy in recent years than any other phase of legislative work. Most legislative activity comprises investigation of some kind. Much investigation, moreover, is directed toward legislative oversight of administrative agencies. John D. Millett has differentiated the following motives for conducting legislative inquiries into administrative action: (1) a public concern; (2) charges of administrative malpractice or inefficiency; (3) personal or political considerations of key legislators; and (4) general political considerations.[9]

Whatever the motives, legislative investigation involves requiring

7 Ralph K. Huitt, "The Roles of Congressional Committee Members," in John C. Wahlke and Heinz Eulau (eds.), *Legislative Behavior* (Glencoe, Ill.: The Free Press, 1959), pp. 317-32, at p. 321.

8 Truman, *op. cit.*, p. 424. "Requests which come to a legislator's office may be referred through his staff to the staff of the bureau. . . . More exceptional ones may give rise to discussion among staff members from the bureau, from a committee, and from individual legislators' offices" (Freeman, *op. cit.*, p. 50). A particularly influential role in agency policy initiation may be played by the ranking committee staff member. *Ibid.*

9 John D. Millett, *Government and Public Administration* (New York: McGraw-Hill Book Co., 1959), pp. 195-96.

administrators to appear before a committee to respond to questions concerning acts of omission or commission. It is true, as Millett observes, that the power of investigation "does not include the power to issue orders or instructions to administrative agencies on the conduct of their operations except as such orders or instructions are embodied in statutory enactment."[10] And Charles S. Hyneman has characterized such direction and control through legislative committees as "spasmodic and uncoordinated."[11] Nevertheless, legislative committees frequently reach far beyond their primary function of framing legislative enactments actually to condition choices, to create situational limits, of particular exercises of administrative discretion in policy initiation. Any administrator who ignores this facet of his external environment, who fails to interact with it willingly and expertly, does so at his own peril.

Individual Legislators

However important committee hearings are for agency policy considerations, the great majority of legislative impingements stems from legislators acting alone or in small groups. Interaction between a legislative committee and an agency may become manifest by interdependencies, understandings, and agreements between a powerful committee chairman and an administrator. Such a situation, which the chairman seeks and the administrator finds tempting, may interdict administrative hierarchy, erode executive responsibility, and weaken intradepartmental hegemony. "The circumstances that contribute to disintegration within the administration and to the dispersion of power within Congress also lead to a diffusion of policy initiative within the administration."[12]

The result is that some committee chairmen become so powerful as to supplant the elected chief executive in the direction and control of at least segments of administration, in spite of the chief executive's

10 *Ibid.*, p. 195.
11 Hyneman, *op. cit. supra,* note 3 at p. 166.
12 Key, "Legislative Control," in Morstein-Marx (ed.), *op. cit.*, p. 322.

constitutional power to "take care that the laws be faithfully executed." The legislator may counter with equal force, particularly with respect to agency policies having the effect of law, that the legislature is constitutionally vested with "all legislative powers." In any case, it is unlikely that this basic conflict of powers within our system of separation of powers ever will be resolved. Indeed, it was intended that power check power. American history confirms that it is in the nature of this separation, and hence this conflict, that a chief executive is weak, or for some reason chooses not to stand his ground against the aggrandizing legislator, it is almost inevitable that the power of the legislator will become augmented at the expense of the power of the chief executive and his administrative subordinates.

Political scientists may never be able to assess fully the awesome power wielded by Senator Joseph R. McCarthy over the Truman and Eisenhower Administrations. A less well-known, though often cited, illustration concerns Representative Carl Vinson of Georgia during his chairmanship, over a twenty-year period, of the House Committee on Naval Affairs, and his subsequent chairmanship of the House Armed Services Committee. His formidable influence over the Navy establishment was extended, after military unification, to include all the armed services, and to such an extent that one Washington journalist described Vinson as "Admiral of the Ocean Seas, Field Marshal of the Armies and, as to the air, Wing Commander of Everything."[13] A Washington rumor had it that on one occasion Chairman Vinson characterized James V. Forrestal as "the best Secretary of the Navy I ever had."[14]

It is doubtful that committee chairmen, and legislators generally, are disposed to perceive limits to the scope of their power in relation to administrative agencies. Seymour Scher describes the congressman's conception of his role as a "representative reviewing agency behavior—a conception that associates him with particular group

[13] William S. White, "Carl Vinson Has Been Unified, Too," *New York Times*, September 1950, p. 12, as quoted and cited in Truman, *op. cit.*, p. 424.
[14] Millett, *op. cit.*, p. 234.

and constituent interests" and involves "no requirement of self-re-straint on his part."[15] Though legislators seek to wield great power over bureaucracy, seldom are their exertions completely successful. Were legislators, collectively and individually, completely effective in their attempts to exert power over administrative agencies, were they really able to maintain control of agency policy making, they would be freer of their frustrations and suspicions concerning the bureauc-racy.[16] Meanwhile, legislators intervene regularly and continually in administrative activity.

Regarding the legislative sector of the government, then, the ad-ministrator must interpret statutes with an eye toward legislative intent, often juggle with contending political and private interests in the arena of the committee hearing, and sensitize his decision making to the wishes and predilections of committee chairmen primarily and legislators generally. But by these activities he does not resolve all the problems affecting his range of choice in policy initiation, for there may be, and often are, other aspects of his environment—and, hence, other problems—that require his interaction or consideration when making a policy decision.

THE ADMINISTRATIVE NETWORK

When making policy decisions, an administrator frequently must in-teract with centers of power and influence within the network of his administrative relationships. These influences, which condition his policy choices, emanate vertically from higher authority, horizontally

[15] Scher, *op. cit.*, pp. 911-20, at p. 912. Administrators of the U. S. Bureau of Indian Affairs, aware of their continuing dependence upon legislative committees, respond to the wishes of their members even with regard to bureau field organiza-tion matters. "For example, the leaders of the Bureau . . . periodically have changed their plans to abolish or transfer some field offices because of protests registered by senior committee members who felt unhappy over the prospect of having Federal installations removed from their home states or districts" (Freeman, *op. cit.*, pp. 49-50).

[16] For an analysis of the legislators' animus toward bureaucracy, see Edward A. Shils, "Resentments and Hostilities of Legislators: Sources, Objects, Consequences," in Wahlke and Eulau (eds.), *op. cit.*, pp. 347-54.

from other agencies, administrators, and jurisdictions, and subordinately from centers and divisions within his organization.

Vertical Influences

An elected chief executive is usually in a position to make special claims upon administrators through executive orders, central controls over jurisdiction, personnel, procurement, and budgeting (which is especially important), and the exercise of other formal management powers, as well as through the energy he brings to the general powers of his office and to his political party leadership.[17]

If the legislature has delegated to the chief executive authority to implement specific programs, he has a formidable influence on policy decisions in those agencies to which he, in turn, entrusts their administration.[18] But even without such express authorizations, his power over administrative agencies, though shared with the legislature and with the judiciary, is substantial.[19]

As a rule, the higher an administrator's position in the hierarchy, the more frequent and direct is the chief executive's influence on his policy decisions. The extent of the chief executive's influence is also affected by the presence or absence of controversy between interest claims concerning policy choices open to the administrator. Although a chief executive usually remains aloof from agency policy issues, in order to avoid alienation of interests, the more controversial such conflicts become the more likely he is to intervene.[20] The size and

17 See, for example, Wallace S. Sayre and Herbert Kaufman, *Governing New York City* (New York: Russell Sage Foundation, 1960), p. 261.

18 Congress is increasingly disposed to delegate lawmaking power to the President. Under the Defense Production Act of 1950, for example, the President is authorized to allocate materials in any way he considers necessary to promote national defense. Not only may he "make rules, regulations, and orders as he deems necessary," but he may delegate his authority to any of a number of officials, departments, and agencies enumerated by the act, according to conditions that he may establish, modify, or withdraw as he sees fit (Public Law No. 774, 81st Cong., 2nd sess., Sept. 8, 1950, sec. 704). For discussion of such delegations, see, for example: John M. Pfiffner and Robert V. Presthus, *Public Administration* (4th ed., New York: The Ronald Press Company, 1960), pp. 540-41; W. Brooke Graves, *Public Administration in a Democratic Society*, pp. 600-2, 605-6.

19 See Truman, *op. cit.*, pp. 426-36.

20 *Ibid.*, pp. 407-9.

complexity of the bureaucracy is a factor: The larger and more heterogeneous system induces greater executive detachment from the numerous issues of administrative policy. Another factor is the amount of organizational autonomy an agency may otherwise experience.

Agency autonomy may stem from functional requirements (technological specialization), restrictions placed upon the chief executive, or lack of stability or continuity of highest political leadership. By legislating directly with respect to suborganizations of departments, legislatures reinforce tendencies toward suborganizational autonomy from vertical influence in decision making. Moreover, agencies created on clientele bases, to reflect special interest groups, are generally less subject to vertical claims than other agencies.[21]

It is apparent, then, that in matters of policy decisions, complete subordination of the administrator to the chief executive—or even to intervening superiors—is rare.

However, in addition to their obvious legal responsibilities to superiors in the hierarchy, administrators often must conciliate and respond to political party leaders. If the administrator's superiors are not themselves party leaders, their relationships with such leaders are usually closer than those of the administrator. Party leaders in the hierarchy can be "redoubtable foes" of an administrator. The influence party leaders attempt to exert on administrative decisions varies. According to Wallace Sayre and Herbert Kaufman, in their monumental study of New York City government, such political influence "relates to the selection or advancement of personnel, or to individual concessions—such as exemptions from formal regulations, dropping prosecutions, hastening the processing of applications—for party followers, members, supporters, and workers. But they may sometimes intervene in broader policy matters also."[22]

21 For an illuminating discussion of interest group influence on organizational autonomy, given a lack of political stability, see Henry W. Ehrmann, "French Bureaucracy and Organized Interests," *Administrative Science Quarterly*, V (March 1961), 534-55. For analysis of how the initiative and creativity of executives, generally, are impeded by methods and procedures needed for coordination, see Marshall E. Dimock, *Administrative Vitality* (New York: Harper & Row, Publishers, 1959), and Melville Dalton, *Men Who Manage* (New York: John Wiley & Sons, Inc., 1959).

22 Sayre and Kaufman, *op. cit. supra*, note 17 at p. 261. See also Chapter 12.

With respect to his superiors, as in his relations with other sectors of his environment, a successful administrator's strategy in policy initiation is, in the words of David B. Truman, one of "constantly attempting to move his activities from a level of controversy to one of acceptance."[23]

Horizontal Influences

Almost all public administration textbooks discuss at length the importance of coordination and communication between and within agencies, and the means by which executives and central staff and control agencies attempt to integrate administrative activity.[24]

Studies of governmental organizations, however, have focused chiefly on relationships within organizations rather than on relationships between them.[25] Though there are exceptions, which emphasize conflict and competition, little attention has been given to examining the ways in which horizontal influences between government agencies affect the exercise of administrative discretion in policy initiation.[26]

After so-called "staff-line" relationships, which have received a great deal of study, are excluded, there remains in every governmental jurisdiction a multitude of horizontal interrelationships that have significant policy implications. A municipal officer suggests a joint community recreation program with a school district. The director of the safety division of a state motor vehicle department proposes a

---

23 Truman, *op. cit.*, p. 447.

24 See, for example, Herbert A. Simon, Donald W. Smithburg, and Victor A. Thompson, *Public Administration* (New York: Alfred A. Knopf, 1950), pp. 166-68 and Chapters 8-14.

25 Studies of interrelationships by sociologists "have largely been confined within the same organizational structure or between a pair of complementary organizations such as management and labor" (Sol Levine and Paul E. White, "Exchange as a Conceptual Framework for the Study of Interorganizational Relationships," *Administrative Science Quarterly*, V [March 1961], 583-601 at p. 584.)

26 For recent studies of interorganizational conflict within government, see, for example: Samuel P. Huntington, "Interservice Competition and the Political Roles of the Armed Services," *American Political Science Review*, LV (March 1961), 40-52; and Marshall E. Dimock, "Expanding Jurisdictions: A Case Study in Bureaucratic Conflict," in Robert K. Merton, Ailsa P. Gray, Barbara Hockey, and Hanan C. Selvin (eds.), *Reader in Bureaucracy* (Glencoe, Ill.: The Free Press, 1952).

new type of school bus to a state superintendent of public instruction. A division of one agency blocks a proposal by another division of the same agency. Assumed capability to perform a specific function of one agency is the crucial element for initiating a proposal in another agency.

It is apparent that an administrator's decision to proceed with or reject a policy idea frequently depends on lateral or horizontal influences exerted by other administrators and agencies. These influences operate both between and within agencies. Difficulty, however, is inherent in the nature of bureaucracy. When a legislature creates a number of agencies and vests each with specific authority, a situation inevitably is created that invites conflicting administrative policies. These conflicts frequently arise from communications difficulties and failures or from absence of coordinating arrangements and procedures. "The individuals who make decisions in the Department of Agriculture cannot possibly know about and take into account everything relating to the price level of the nation which the individuals in the Federal Trade Commission and the individuals in the Federal Reserve Board know about and take into account."[27] Nevertheless, what one agency decides to do may vitally affect what other agencies are doing. This spells a dilemma for the administrator.[28]

The larger and the more complex the bureaucracy is, the more difficult it is for an administrator to keep informed of. and to respond to, related administrative activity elsewhere. To make always what Herbert Simon has termed "satisficing" decisions in policy initiation,

[27] Hyneman, *op. cit.*, p. 445.

[28] "In various areas . . . agency policies must be coordinated and welded into an integrated whole. Certain areas such as transportation, communication and energy are obvious areas where such coordination is essential" (James M. Landis, *Report on Regulatory Agencies to the President-Elect* [Washington, D. C.: U. S. Gov't. Printing Office, 1960], p. 74). For discussion of "the most ambitious effort yet made to coordinate policy on the cabinet level in American federal government," see Paul Y. Hammond, "The National Security Council as a Device for Interdepartmental Coordination: An Interpretation and Appraisal," *American Political Science Review*, LIV (December 1960), 899-910. Alleged failures in coordination evoked widespread criticism in the dramatic controversies surrounding U. S. government efforts concerning the 1960 "U-2 incident" and the 1961 'Cuban invasion" attempt.

the administrator must be able to interact skillfully with the horizontal influences in the administrative network that surrounds him.[29]

Subordinate Influences

The behavior of personnel within an agency is also crucial to policy decisions. What an administrator proposes to do—making his choice from among policy alternatives—is largely dependent upon his subordinates. The way in which he manages these decision-making or goal-setting relationships will have a major impact upon the quality of leadership he gives to the enterprise.

It is in the nature of large-scale organizations, however, for conflicts concerning policy choices to arise among internal interest groups. Competition among suborganizations requires the continuing attention of leadership. Conflicting loyalties and values find a social base in the group structure of the enterprise.[30]

[29] "While economic man maximizes—selects the best alternative from among all those available to him; his cousin, whom we shall call administrative man, satisfices—looks for a course of action that is satisfactory or 'good enough' " (Herbert A. Simon, *Administrative Behavior* [2nd ed.; New York: The Macmillan Co., 1957], p. xxv). Simon develops his concept of "administrative man" as one of "limited rationality" in his *Models of Man* (New York: John Wiley & Sons, Inc., 1957), especially Chapters 14, 15, and, with James G. March, in a chapter entitled "Cognitive Limits on Rationality," in *Organizations* (New York: John Wiley & Sons, Inc., 1958), p. 137. For findings and commentaries that tend to confirm Simon's concept, see Nicholas G. Nicolaidis, *Policy-Decision and Organization Theory* (unpublished doctoral dissertation, University of Southern California School of Public Administration, 1960); John M. Pfiffner, "Administrative Rationality," *Public Administration Review*, XX (Summer 1960), 125-32; and Charles E. Lindblom, "The Science of 'Muddling Through,' " *Public Administration Review*, XIX (Spring 1959), 79-88. James D. Thompson has suggested that the concept of decision-making man as a satisficer rather than as a maximizer has utility in distinguishing "leadership" from mere "headship" in administration. See his "Leadership and Administration: Competing or Complementary Concepts?" unpublished paper delivered at the 1958 Annual Meeting of the American Political Science Association, September 4-6, 1958, mimeographed, p. 9.

[30] Philip Selznick, *Leadership in Administration* (Evanston: Row, 1957), pp. 63, 94. "If the policies that originate within the administrative organization are formulated and put into effect by its several divisions, we are bound to end up with conflicting policies" (Hyneman, *op. cit.*, p. 446). James D. Thompson has helped elucidate the causes of such intraorganizational conflicts, i.e., differences of administrative allocations, latent roles of the labor force, and competing pressures arising from differences in the task environment. See his "Organizational Man-

Sociologists Ohlin and Pappenfort have demonstrated that internal conflicts can be ideological. In their study of organizational change within public correctional administration, they describe how adherents of a welfare ideology, social workers, may engender a "public crisis" by enlisting outside community support to oppose successfully adherents of a protective ideology, the administrators.[31]

Chris Argyris has observed that the very nature of formal organization causes the subordinate at any given level to experience "competition, rivalry, intersubordinate hostility, and to develop a focus toward the parts rather than the whole."[32] In other words, recent research makes it clear that formal organization requirements conflict with internal individual and group needs.[33]

---

agement of Conflict," *Administrative Science Quarterly*, IV (March 1960), 389-409. "Whatever the form of organization, the differences in the aggregate activities is probably far less significant than the differences of grouping and hence of interaction required of members" (*ibid.*, p. 392). By implication, Thompson elsewhere suggests technological development as still another cause, i.e., increasing technological specialization increases the likelihood that organizational members owe greater allegiance to their professions than to organizational demands, hence greater opportunity for conflict between the two—"for the individual employee to enforce demands on the organization by invoking sanctions from the profession" and "for organizational members to differentiate among themselves and hence for cleavage to develop"; see his and Frederick L. Bates's "Technology, Organization, and Administration," *Administrative Science Quarterly*, II (December 1957), 325-43, at p. 343.

31 "For example, in a midwestern system one faction of probation-parole agents supplied critics outside the agency with information which was used against the organization" (Lloyd E. Ohlin and Donnell M. Pappenfort, "Crisis, Succession, and Organizational Change," an unpublished and undated paper, mimeographed, p. 5).

32 Chris Argyris, "The Individual and Organization: Some Problems of Mutual Adjustment," *Administrative Science Quarterly*, II (June 1957), 1-25, at p. 22. See also his *Personality and Organization* (New York: Harper & Row, Publishers, 1957). For popular commentaries on conflict between individual needs and organizational demands, see, for example, William H. Whyte, *The Organization Man* (New York: Simon and Schuster, Inc., 1956); and David Riesman, *The Lonely Crowd* (New Haven: Yale University Press, 1950).

33 The analysis of small groups in organizations is receiving increasing attention in sociological research. See, for example, Nicholas J. Demerath and John W. Thibaut, "Small Groups and Administrative Organizations," *Administrative Science Quarterly*, I (September 1956), 139-54; and Peter M. Blau, "Patterns of Interaction Among a Group of Officials in a Government Agency," in Albert H. Rubenstein and Chadwick J. Haberstroh (eds.), *Some Theories of Organization* (Homewood, Ill.: Richard D. Irwin, 1960), pp. 299-310.

The needs of subordinates and the demands of organization constitute a perennial and fundamental dilemma for the administrator in the process of making policy decisions. The problem is especially significant for the administrator of a government agency, since he is beset with manifold and complex pressures from every direction—from within the administrative network, from the legislature, and from his agency's even less structured nongovernmental environment. One may wonder how it is possible for the public administrator to select and initiate reasonable policy proposals when he is in a constant state of suspension within this unpredictable and changing social milieu.

NONGOVERNMENTAL PRESSURES

When General E. R. Quesada was appointed Administrator of the Federal Aviation Agency in 1958, he was prepared for resistance, arguments, and delays. But he was not prepared for "the sustained, highly organized pressure campaigns" that he soon encountered at every turn. Nor did he anticipate that his own motives, and those of his agency, would be, as he said, "constantly questioned, that the Congress and the public would be deliberately misled and misinformed, and that willful misrepresentations would be used to stir up grievances and foment resentment among the very men whose own lives were at stake in our own safety rules." He attributed his trials and tribulations to two pressure groups—the Aircraft Owners and Pilots Association and the Air Line Pilots Association. And so, as he neared retirement in January 1961, General Quesada lashed back at these "irresponsible" and "intemperate" organizations in an article published in *Harper's*.[34]

Political scientists might well respond that the General should not have been so surprised at what awaited him, for they have long recognized the pervasiveness and power of private pressures in the shaping of public policy. Indeed, Latham, Truman, and many others have

[34] E. R. Quesada, "The Pressures Against Air Safety," *Harper's Magazine*, CCXXII, No. 58 (January 1961), 58-64, at p. 58.

stated the essence of the governmental process in these terms.[35] Though only in recent years have organizational studies by sociologists dealt with relations between organizations and external social units,[36] political science literature has been replete with such emphasis since Arthur F. Bentley published his seminal study of politics in 1908.[37] And most students of public administration, including such distinguished contributors as Herring, Leiserson, Gaus, and Appleby, have long taken into account the importance of the interest group in the administrative process of government.[38]

Interest group activity in public administration is so omnipresent and diverse that it resists attempts toward simplification and orderly classification. Our purpose here, therefore, is not to distinguish all the manifold facets of interest-group activity that may bear on agency policy initiation, but rather to isolate problems confronting the administrator in connection with three important aspects of the subject: (1) representation and access; (2) external research; and (3) multiplicity of values.

Representation and Access

Policy initiation by external interest groups frequently occurs through interest representation that has been built into the bureaucratic structure. The usual means by which interest access to agency

35 See, for example, Latham, *op. cit* ; Truman, *op. cit.*; and Donald C. Blaisdell, *American Democracy Under Pressure* (New York: The Ronald Press Company, 1957). For classics on this subject, one must, of course, refer to James Madison's famous tenth number of *The Federalist* (1788) and to John C. Calhoun's *Disquisition on Government* (1851).

36 Amitai Etzioni, "New Directions in the Study of Organizations and Society," *Social Research,* XXVII (Summer 1960), 223-28, at p. 223.

37 Arthur F. Bentley, *The Process of Government, A Study of Social Pressures* (Chicago, 1908; reissued Bloomington: Chicago University Press, 1949). For recent commentaries on Bentley's influence, see R. E. Dowling, "Pressure Group Theory: Its Methodological Range," Myron Q. Hale, "The Cosmology of Arthur F. Bentley," and Robert T. Golembiewski, " 'The Group Basis of Politics': Notes on Analysis and Development," in "Bentley Revisited," *American Political Science Review,* LIV (December 1960), 944-71.

38 See, for example, Herring, *Public Administration and the Public Interest*; Leiserson, *Administrative Regulation: A Study in Representation of Interests*; John M. Gaus, *Reflections on Public Administration* (University, Ala.: University of Alabama Press, 1947); and Paul H. Appleby, *Policy and Administration.*

decision making becomes institutionalized and legitimatized within the official structure of administration are these: An agency is created to serve the interest; interest-group members are appointed to administrative positions; a plural-headed form of agency organization is employed to accommodate interest representation within the apex of the structure. Thus, Avery Leiserson discusses interest groups in administration in terms of clientele organizations, staffing for a point of view, and interest representation on administrative boards.[39] And, incidentally, such practices are not limited to the United States.[40]

Agency creation.   Many agencies are created by legislatures with the express or implied intent that they serve particular clienteles or interest groups. "The prevailing practice is that the administrative agencies represent the interests they serve."[41] It is indeed a rare circumstance, therefore, for the Veterans Administration to oppose the interests of veterans, for the Department of Agriculture to oppose the interests of farmers, for the Army Corps of Engineers to act contrary to inland river and harbor interests, or for a fair employment practices commission to block the interests of ethnic minority groups. Moreover, this tendency may be present even in agencies created to regulate groups, as distinguished from those created to render services or benefits. Since, as experience indicates, regulated groups have more cohesion than those demanding regulation, little is done by an independent regulatory commission beyond what is "acceptable" to the regulated groups.[42]

The administrator of a so-called "clientele" agency has the continuing problem of assessing the changing pressure from the external group environment of his agency. At the maximum, the legislature has ordained that he act as a bureaucratic representative of such groups, that he translate group pressures into public policy by the

[39] Avery Leiserson, "Interest Groups in Administration," in Morstein-Marx (ed.), *op. cit.*, pp. 294-311, 297-309.

[40] See Henry W. Ehrmann (ed.), *Interest Groups on Four Continents* (Pittsburgh: University of Pittsburgh Press, 1958), pp. 269-89, and his "French Bureaucracy and Organized Interests," *op. cit.*

[41] Key. *Politics, Parties, and Pressure Groups*, p. 724.

[42] Truman, *op. cit.*, p. 418.

exercise of his agency's discretion. At the minimum, he is peculiarly vulnerable to policy initiation from groups he serves or regulates. In clientele agencies, "access" can vary from merely making group interests known to actual decision making.

Appointment. Though patronage is usually dispensed through political party machinery as a reward for successful party activity, appointments to administrative positions also may reflect efforts to secure interest group representation in the bureaucracy. Agencies are frequently staffed with interest representatives in order to bring the points of view of external social units into policy initiation and formulation. This practice may simultaneously serve party patronage considerations, for a person may become politically "available" for such a position by virtue of his dual role of party workhorse and representative of a particular interest. But even in classified, as distinguished from patronage, positions, interest representation need not be incompatible with so-called merit appointments. Nor must the interest representative in bureaucracy necessarily forsake his interest group allegiance by virtue of his merit appointment. Indeed, his ability to fulfill the purpose of his appointment, his usefulness in government, may turn on his continuing to maintain his interest contacts.

One should recognize, however, that the disadvantages of such a practice may far outweigh the advantages. Leiserson points out several possible dangers as, for example, conflicting loyalties, difficulties of coordination and control, outside access to inside information, and emotional and physical strains upon the interest group representative. He would exclude the practice from operating and technical levels.[43]

Whatever the dangers, the practice of appointing external group representatives to administrative positions is prevalent and sometimes beyond the control of certain administrators. It is not extraordinary, therefore, for an administrator to find agency policy decisions circumscribed by the incumbencies of interest representatives whose representative roles persist after appointment. It is also worth noting

[43] Leiserson, "Interest Groups in Administration," in Morstein-Marx (ed.), *op. cit.*, pp. 302-5.

that when such representatives, as well as others on agency payrolls, become "educated" in agency expertise and processes, and subsequently are employed by external interest groups with which the agency interacts, they thereby may enhance interest group ability to influence agency policy initiation. It is difficult to overstate the extent and policy impact of personnel exchange between agencies and the groups that comprise their nongovernmental environment.

A host of problems may result from the appointment of interest group representatives, especially for the administrator at those critical moments when he must decide whether to accept policy proposals for possible adoption. His basic problem is how best to utilize interest group representatives for policy ideas without permitting them to abuse or pervert agency responsibilities and goals.

Plural-headed agencies.   A controversy has raged for many years within the literature of public administration between those who would "reform" administration by centralizing, simplifying, and unifying administration and those who have been skeptical of such cure-alls. Dwight Waldo, in tracing this controversy, has observed: "The case for centralization seemed so clear, so indubitable, that the measures by which it was prescribed and applied seemed to be 'principles,' of universal validity, comparable to the Golden Rule, or an axiom from Euclid, or both. And so were born the 'canons of integration,' the 'dogmas of centralization.' "[44] Advocates of centralization frequently argue that all boards and commissions should be abolished. Thus, in 1950, Connecticut's "Little Hoover Commission" recommended:

> Good management requires that all administrative powers at each level in an organization be in the hands of one man. This is indispensable to any clear responsibility for results, and to prevent opportunities for "passing the buck." It is for this reason that we have recommended that each department, without exception, be headed by a single Commissioner, not by a board.[45]

[44] Dwight Waldo, *The Administrative State* (New York: Ronald Press Co., 1948), p. 133. See Chapter 8, entitled "Centralization vs. Decentralization," and the writers cited therein.

[45] *The Report of the Commission on State Government Organization to the General Assembly and the Governor of Connecticut* (Pursuant to Special Act. No. 28, 1949 Session of the Connecticut General Assembly), p. 34.

This recommendation was ignored by Connecticut's General Assembly.

The fact is that three generic forms or models of agency organization are widely employed in public administration: the single head; the full-time board or commission; and the part-time policy board or commission with a full-time administrator responsible to it. The effectiveness of each is situational; each has its advantages and disadvantages.[46] Only plural-headed forms, however, institutionalize policy making by interest group representatives at the apex of agency structure.

In the full-time board or commission form, three or more full-time administrators with staggered terms constitute top management. When there is a part-time board with a full-time administrator, a fairly large board with staggered terms, acting on a part-time basis, makes top agency policy decisions and hears appeals, while the full-time administrator carries out the program. Most regulatory commissions and government corporations are variants of one or the other of these two forms, but in some jurisdictions the plural-headed agency is used much more extensively. For example, of some eighty-two Wisconsin state administrative agencies, twenty-two have single heads, six have full-time boards or commissions, and fifty-four have part-time boards or commissions, two of the latter being selected by interest groups having no official connection with the state government.[47]

Statutes vary in the detail with which they specify the interests to be represented on the full-time and part-time boards or commissions. In some instances, either by choice or by statutory requirement, the chief executive appoints as members those nominated by the groups represented. This is the method by which most state professional examining and licensing boards are appointed, and it is often tantamount to complete delegation of policy-making authority to non-

46 See, for example Wisconsin Legislative Reference Library, *A Basic Study of Administrative Organization of the State of Wisconsin* (Informational Bulletin No. 148 [Madison, Wisc.: State Capitol], February 1956), p. 13.
47 *Ibid.*, p. 19.

governmental interests or associations.[48] That interest groups are more influential in initiating policy with plural-headed, as against single-headed, forms is an unproved though reasonable inference.

The impact upon administrators of policy initiation from non-governmental pressures represented on boards or commissions is frequently immediate and direct. What otherwise would be a problem of external interaction with interest groups becomes compounded by being a problem of internal as well as external interaction. And administrators may be continually threatened with losing policy initiative entirely to the social units that they are charged with serving or regulating. Whether results are favorable chiefly depends upon the situational wisdom of the legislature in resorting to such forms and upon the qualities of the personnel involved—both board members and administrators.[49]

External Research

When the Federal Communications Commission receives a technical proposal from the Radio Corporation of America, or from some other electronics firm, which, if adopted, would require promulgation of a rule affecting the nation's television industry, the commission must evaluate the proposal. But even though the quality of television and huge sums of money may be involved, the FCC does not have engineers or specialists on its staff—nor the appropriations to hire them—sufficiently competitive in quality with RCA's highly paid research and development staff to enable the commission to determine whether the proposal is desirable or efficacious. Accordingly, the FCC regularly submits such proposals to its all-industry advisory

[48] Leiserson, "Interest Groups in Administration," in Morstein-Marx (ed.), *op. cit.*, p 306.

[49] Of all the criticisms of the federal regulatory boards and commissions made by James M. Landis, perhaps none overshadows his remarks on personnel: "It is generally admitted by most observers that since World War II a deterioration in the quality of our administrative personnel has taken place, both at the top level and throughout the staff." And he added: "The prime key to the improvement of the administrative process is the selection of qualified personnel. Good men can make poor laws workable; poor men will wreak havoc with good laws" (James M. Landis, *Report on Regulatory Agencies to President-Elect*, pp. 11, 66).

committee in the hope that the technical staffs of competing firms may act, if necessary, as a countervailing influence in the policy-initiation process. No one on the advisory committee represents the viewing public. The result in such instances is that the FCC becomes a captive of the television industry, particularly of the research and development staffs of the firms comprising the industry that the FCC is charged with regulating.[50]

So highly technical and complex has much of public administration become that most major federal government agencies find it impossible to retain on a full-time basis the variety of scientific advisors needed. Not only do some agencies, therefore, become overwhelmingly dependent on external advice, as in the case of the FCC, but many agencies contract research and development programs with outside interests, and otherwise depend on outside technology and research resources, thus multiplying greatly opportunities for policy initiative by outside interests. Prior to 1940, most federal government research was done within the government, but by 1953 only 25 per cent continued to be done by government agencies. Meanwhile, federal expenditures for scientific research and development had increased 22 times, 90 per cent of the total being expended for applied research and development.[51]

Nongovernmental research groups have also become important in the legislative branch. Of thirteen studies on U.S. foreign policy prepared in 1960 as "background material" for the U.S. Senate Foreign Relations Committee's sweeping review of foreign policy, only one was prepared by the committee's staff. The remaining twelve were prepared by outside organizations, including eight universities.[52]

[50] I am indebted to Thomas M. Cooley II, long familiar with FCC processes, for focusing my attention upon this problem. " 'Research policy is made in a political context.' Research . . . must reflect an established adjustment among group interests if it is to be carried on. Whether or not an administrative agency can do particular types of research is in part a reflection of the relative position of the group interests that impinge upon the agency" (Truman, *op. cit.*, p. 446).

[51] Alan C. Rankin, "Administrative Processes of Contract and Grant Research," *Administrative Science Quarterly*, I (December 1956), 275-94, at pp. 275, 276, 287.

[52] See Committee on Foreign Relations, United States Senate, *United States Foreign Policy, Compilation of Studies* (87th Cong., 1st sess., document 24) (Washington, D. C.: U. S. Gov't. Printing Office, March 14, 1961), pp. iv, vii; hereafter cited as U. S. Senate, *United States Foreign Policy* (1961).

The enormous extent of governmental dependence for policy initiative on external research and technological development becomes evident only when recent expenditures for these functions in higher education and industry are examined. In 1957, the federal government spent $916 million on research, of which $602 million was expended in the physical sciences, $278 million in the life sciences, and $36 million in the social sciences. Most of the research was conducted outside the government. In 1953-54, separately budgeted research expenditures in U.S. colleges and universities totaled $205 million, of which 65 per cent was contributed by the federal government.[53] The National Science Foundation has reported that during 1958 almost 70,000 scientists and engineers, or 44 per cent of the total at U.S. colleges and universities, were engaged in research and development that represented an allocation of $736 million in the 377 reporting colleges and universities.[54] It was estimated that in 1960 approximately one-fourth of the entire budget for U.S. higher education was being financed by the federal government in the form of funds for scientific research and science education.[55]

Expenditures by U.S. industry are even more impressive. In 1956, private industry expended an estimated $6.5 *billion* on research and development in the natural sciences and engineering.[56] It is estimated that private industry is spending only $137 million annually on social science research, of which some $125 million is for opinion and attitude surveys and marketing research.[57]

If, as predicted, approximately $120 billion is spent on research and development in the United States between 1960 and 1970, the nation's total investment in science and technology from 1776 to 1960

53 *Ibid.*, pp. 112, 113.

54 The Pittsburgh *Press,* May 29, 1961, p. 5.

55 Bentley Glass, "The Academic Scientist: 1940-1960," *AAUP Bulletin,* XLVI (June 1960), 149-155, at p. 152; "Professional workers in science and technology now . . . constitute about 30 per cent of the entire professional element of our population (6 to 7 million persons)" (*ibid.,* p. 150).

56 National Science Foundation, *Reviews of Data on Research and Development,* No. 10 (Washington, D. C.: U. S. Gov't. Printing Office, 1958), p. 1.

57 Harry Alpert, "The Growth of Social Research in the United States," in Donald Lerner (ed.), *The Human Meaning of the Social Sciences* (New York: Meridian Books, Inc., 1959), pp. 73-86.

will be substantially exceeded.[58] Already, about 500,000 articles are published in U.S. scientific journals each year.[59]

The present allocation of scientific research and development is overwhelmingly toward military needs, with the physical sciences first in emphasis, the biological sciences second, and the social sciences very far behind.[60] Approximately 10 per cent of the U.S. gross national product is devoted to military purposes. The arms race consumes 50 per cent of U.S. research and development efforts. "And the rapid changes in military technology are pushing the expenditures of money and research effort continually higher."[61]

Social scientists have almost ignored the significance of nongovernmental research and technological development for policy initiation in public administration. Yet it is doubtful that the rapid growth of this influence can be overstated. Nongovernmental research organizations reflect special interests much the same as do pressure groups. Even in state and local government, the dependence on external research is becoming major rather than incidental. Political scientist Edward F. Cooke has warned that such a trend "bodes ill for our democratic processes" and threatens to make "a travesty" of representative government.[62]

The problems posed for public administrators are more specific. Poor coordination of information among agencies is not unusual. Some agencies must rely entirely on information passed on to them by nongovernmental interest groups. Labor unions, small business,

58 Francis Bello, "The 1960's: A Forecast of the Technology," *Fortune* (January 1959), p. 200. In 1959, "over 10 billions of dollars were spent in the United States for research and development" (Glass, *op. cit.*, pp. 149-155, at pp. 151-152).

59 U. S. Senate, *United States Foreign Policy*, p. 166.

60 *Ibid.*, p. 101; see also pp. 111-13.

61 Harrison Brown, "The Prospective Environment for Policymaking and Administration," in U. S. Senate, *United States Foreign Policy*, Appendix A, pp. 937-959, at p. 951.

62 Edward F. Cooke, "Research: An Instrument of Political Power," *Political Science Quarterly*, LXXVI (March 1961), 69-87, at pp. 85, 87. Cooke presents evidence showing that the research weapon has brought the Pennsylvania Economy League, in its capacity as a fact gatherer, into the inner circle of decision makers of Pennsylvania state and local governments. "The evidence shows that the PEL has been a formulator of public policy; in some instances it has been responsible also for the administration of its own proposals" (*ibid.*, p. 85).

and other interests are generally at a disadvantage in comparison with wealthier interests because they possess relatively meager research and statistical services. It is not easy for an administrator to prevent his dependence upon information-supplying interests from prejudicing other interests; his policy decisions may reflect a built-in bias of his structured research relationships with outside groups.[63]

Henry A. Kissinger suggests an even more basic problem for the public administrator, one that arises from a possible conflict between the mode of policy and the mode of analysis or research. The difference is one of perspective. After recognizing "the inevitable element of conjecture in policymaking," Kissinger observes:

> Effective policy fits its measures to circumstances. Analysis strives to eliminate the accidental; it seeks principles of general validity. . . . Policy looks toward the future; its pace is dictated by the need for decision in a finite time. Analysis assumes an accomplished act or a given set of factors; its pace is the pace of reflection.[64]

The making of qualitative policy decisions requires the adjustment of these differences. The problem becomes aggravated as the increasing scope and complexity of government make it necessary for policy initiatives to be supported by thoughtful analysis and research by outside interests.

Perhaps the greatest problem facing administrators who must depend on external research is the threat of deprivation of control of the policy-making process. "As a technology becomes elongated, any particular organization will tend to have less control over the total technological process, to be more dependent on other organizations for prior or subsequent operations in the total process." Such a development "tends to reduce flexibility in deciding goals and managing resources."[65]

The crucial fact underlying all problems connected with the impingements of external research on agency policy decisions is that

---

[63] For confirmation that similar problems exist in French administration, see Ehrmann, "French Bureaucracy and Organized Interests," pp. 545-46.

[64] Henry A. Kissinger, "The Policymaker and the Intellectual," *The Reporter*, XX (March 5, 1959), 30-35, at p. 34.

[65] Thompson and Bates, *op. cit.*, pp. 325-43, at p. 343.

modern commitments of government require public administrators to defer to expertise, and that when public agencies do not command the necessary expertise within their own ranks, reliance upon non-governmental resources and interests becomes imperative. The public administrator's task, in essence, is to fit external research and technology to policy decisions that serve, rather than pervert, agency purposes and goals.

Multiplicity of Values

The interests of men are exceedingly diverse. "Many men have many minds," R. M. MacIver has observed, and "the attitudes of every group differ from the attitudes of every other."[66] Some philosophers attribute heterogeneity of thought and behavior, as well as the tendency to associate in groups, to the "nature" of man, a euphemism occasionally resorted to when rational explanation is found wanting. John Dewey merely dismissed the question how or why individuals become associated as having no sense. "If there is any mystery about the matter," he wrote, "it is the mystery that the universe is the kind of universe it is."[67] The question is one for philosophers, among others. But the existence of a multiplicity of both governmental and nongovernmental values and pressures is an indisputable fact with which public administrators must contend when making policy decisions.

Government agencies must constantly respond to a vast assortment of stimuli in policy initiation. Charlton Ogburn provides an outstanding illustration—of necessity a lengthy one—by describing a sample of the demands made of the Department of State in a typical day:

> A new Soviet threat to Berlin, a forthcoming conference of Foreign Ministers of the Organization of American States, a request from Poland for credit, a solicitation for support of a candidacy for the Presidency of the United Nations General Assembly, a plea from an ambassador that

[66] R. M. MacIver, *The Web of Government* (New York: The Macmillan Company, 1947), p. 422.

[67] John Dewey, *The Public and Its Problems* (Chicago: Gateway Books, 1946), p. 23.

the head of the government to which he is accredited be invited to visit the United States officially, a refusal by another government to permit the duty-free importation of some official supplies for a U. S. consulate, a request from the White House for comment on the foreign affairs section of a major presidential address, an earthquake in the Aegean creating hardships which it appears the U. S. Navy might be able to alleviate, a request for a speaker from a foreign policy association in California, a transmittal slip from a member of Congress asking for information with which to reply to a letter from a constituent protesting discriminatory actions against his business by a foreign government, letters from citizens both supporting and deploring the policy of nonrecognition of Communist China, a continuing inquiry by a press correspondent who has got wind of a top secret telegram from Embassy Bonn on the subject of German rearmament and is determined to find out what is in it, a demand by a Protestant church group that the Department take steps to prevent harassment of their coreligionists in a foreign country, a request by a delegation of a federation of women's clubs for a briefing on southeast Asia and suggestions as to how its members might be useful in their planned tour of the area, a request from Consulate General Brazzaville for a revision of cost-of-living allowances, a visit by a commission of inquiry into the operations of U. S. foreign aid programs, a notification from the staff of the National Security Council that a revision of the National Security Council paper on dependent areas is due, a telegram from a U. S. embassy in the Near East declaring that last night's flareups make a visit by the Assistant Secretary for Near Eastern and South Asian Affairs, now in mid-Atlantic, inopportune at the moment, a warning by a European Foreign Minister of the consequences should the United States fail to support his nation's position in the Security Council, and a counterwarning by an African representative at the United Nations of the consequences should the United States do so. . . .[68]

The Department of State, of course, must respond to a worldwide mosaic of interactions. But agencies with much narrower jurisdictions are also subjected to multiple pressures from their extra-governmental environments.

[68] Charlton Ogburn, Jr., "The Flow of Policymaking in the Department of State," in U. S. Senate, *United States Foreign Policy*, pp. 970-75, at p. 970. This sample does not include "the oceans of informational reports that come into the Department by telegram and air pouch or the countless periodicals from all parts of the world that arrive by sea" (*ibid.*).

After studying the processes of 332 policy decisions, the great majority of them in state and local government agencies, one writer concluded: "The organizational environment, and particularly the organization clientele, is a storage of forces which exercises noteworthy influences in shaping organization policies."[69]

William Gore's analysis of thirty-three policy decisions in eighteen federal field offices in the state of Washington stresses the importance in policy initiation of (1) agency reliance upon information from external sources; (2) "incompatible demands" from outside interests; and (3) agency role conception as warring with competitive private interests. In every instance, agency administrators regarded themselves as subjected to demands that conflicted with agency goals or with the demands of other external groups.[70]

Robert Hawkes has demonstrated that the role of the administrator in a state psychiatric hospital is a product, and a part, of three interdependent and overlapping "social subsystems," each characterized by specific mores and socioeconomic attributes: (1) the system of economic and political support, involving the administrator's interaction with such "outside" persons as a board of trustees, and "marked by the input of money and organizational authority for the administrator"; (2) the system of medicine and its related professions, involving his interaction with medical groups outside the hospital, and marked by the input of personnel, approved treatment procedures, and medical authority; and (3) the community system that provides the hospital with patients, involving interaction between hospital staff and problem population, and marked by patient admission and discharge.[71]

Even during World War II, when the existence of the nation itself was in great jeopardy, differences among nongovernmental pressures were not always subordinated to national needs. Bela Gold's study of wartime economic planning in agriculture attributed differences

[69] Nicolaidis, *op. cit.*, p. 90.

[70] William J. Gore, "Administrative Decision-Making in Federal Field Offices," *Public Administration Review*, XVI (Autumn 1956), 281-91.

[71] Robert W. Hawkes, "The Role of the Psychiatric Administrator," *Administrative Science Quarterly*, VI (June 1961), 89-106.

among farmers to the factors of geographic location, the relative scale of farming operations, and product differentiation. "The particular loyalties engendered by sheer geographical location had their most direct bearing, of course, on the issues of modifying the regional distribution of farm labor, agricultural machinery and fertilizers." Moreover, industries competing with agriculture for productive resources "were bent on reducing its allocations of manpower, materials, machinery components and manufacturing facilities." When there was cooperation between industrial groups and government officials in meeting mobilization needs, it generally materialized only from the direct economic interests of the groups involved. "Instances in which such co-operation was voluntarily forthcoming, in spite of prospective substantial disadvantage to those taking part, were strikingly less common." The consuming public, on the other hand, played only a minor role in policy initiation, probably because of the absence of overt consumer pressures. Thus, Gold characterized governmental action as representing "a congeries of cooperating, competing and conflicting interests."[72]

It can be said, then, that public administrators at every level are enveloped by a matrix of contending policy initiators consisting of three interdependent and interacting sectors—the legislature, the administrative network, and the nongovernmental environment. Public administration is marked by multiple points of access, which reproduce a bewildering array of problems in the never-ending process of policy initiation. The process of initiation is interlaced with inherent conflict which, if chaos is to be avoided, must be carefully managed.

[72] Bela Gold, *Wartime Economic Planning in Agriculture* (New York: Columbia University Press, 1949), pp. 507, 519-20, 512, 521.

Chapter Three

Public
Participation

Initiation and public participation are the most important policy-making stages, substantively, and the most complex, procedurally, because they involve interaction of administrators with centers of power and influence outside the agency.

As we have observed, individuals or organizations of the outside public may become involved in several stages of the policy-making process. We know that an administrator must get his ideas for policy proposals from somewhere, and that private interests are among his principal sources. As discussed in Chapter 2, this process of initiation is interlaced with inherent conflict deriving in major part from nongovernmental pressures. But once an administrator has decided to proceed with a policy idea, and the idea has become crystallized into a tentatively drafted agency proposal, he may then decide to elicit advice of the interested or prospectively affected public by employing certain techniques—principally informal conferences, advisory committees, and public hearings. If he does so, then public participation becomes a distinguishable stage of policy formulation. It also becomes an important stage in terms of bureaucratic responsibility, the idea of government by consent, or democratic theory generally. Though participative techniques are broadly identified in our discussion of the policy-making cycle in Chapter 1, they remain to be evaluated in this chapter.

Every set of circumstances for agency policy making is unique. An administrator who wants to elicit effective public participation must be cognizant of the advantages and disadvantages of each technique available to him. Indiscriminate use or structuring of public participation techniques will prejudice his attainment of agency objectives.[1] After all, such techniques are merely means of accomplishing policy goals.

INFORMAL CONFERENCES OR CONSULTATIONS

What, then, are the advantages and disadvantages of the informal conference or consultation of which the astute administrator should be mindful?

Some of its *advantages* are:

1. Persons who are not accustomed to public speaking and formal procedures are more likely to present facts and opinions at an informal conference, or upon personal contact with the administrator, than at a formal public hearing.

2. The technique is especially suited for obtaining factual information of a highly technical character.

3. Informal conferences or consultations prior to a public hearing often clarify issues and thereby facilitate conduct of the public hearing. In this respect, they may serve somewhat the same functions that pre-trial conferences serve in relation to judicial proceedings.

4. The personal relationships developed between the administrator and affected interests during an informal conference or consulta-

---

[1] For writings that emphasize such perils, see, for example, Emmette S. Redford, "The Protection of the Public Interest with Special Reference to Administrative Regulation," *American Political Science Review*, XLVIII (December 1954), 1,103-13; Leiserson, *Administrative Regulation: A Study in Representation of Interests;* Donn R. Grandpré, "Let's Have a Conference," *Personnel Administration*, XXIII (July-August 1960), 4-9; Henry A. Kissinger, "The Policymaker and the Intellectual," *The Reporter*, XX (March 5, 1959), 30-35.

tion often facilitate subsequent enforcement and acceptance of the policy.

Some *disadvantages* are:

1. Information obtained at a conference may be inaccurate, and opinions may be unrepresentative, especially if the conference involves only one person or interest.

2. The procedure tends to be effective only if there is an organized group or interest to contact.

3. There is a danger that a highly vocal group will exert influence that is disproportionate to its numbers and interests.

Despite its disadvantages, the informal conference or consultation serves an administrator as both a fact-finding and a public relations device and is utilized in the policy-making process of every administrative agency of government.[2] Weaknesses of the technique are readily overcome. Administrators frequently check information obtained from a conference with only one interest against the information provided by opposing interests. When an administrator remains unsatisfied with his use of this technique in a particular situation, he often supplements it with an advisory committee meeting or a subsequent public hearing at which information obtained at the informal conference is made known to all interested persons. One of the prime virtues of the informal conference or consultation is flexibility. It can and should be tailored to fit the needs of each particular situation. It is unwise, therefore, for a legislature to prescribe its use in any way.

ADVISORY COMMITTEES

A Struggle for Power

Not all students of public administration agree that advisory committees are desirable. Such committees have been berated as devices to subvert or destroy democratic administration. Detractors view ad-

[2] For appraisal of British use of conference and committee techniques, see John Cohen, "Study of Committees and Conferences," *Public Administration*, XXX (Winter 1952), 361-67.

visory committees as time-wasting diffusers of legally reposed administrative authority and responsibility. They allege that such committees serve as convenient channels for favoritism—for those interests represented to exert power over administrators and, through them, over those interests that are not so represented. These and other charges apparently derive from some social theory that stresses a perennial struggle for power among social groups.[3]

Proper use and structuring of advisory committees can obviate charges made by critics. Many alleged disadvantages are eliminated by cautious techniques of appointment and the exercise of leadership by administrators.

By depending too much on an advisory committee, it is argued, an administrator may lose control of policy initiative and the decision process to the co-opted representatives of outside interests comprising the committee. The administrator serves the committee, rather than the converse. If advisory committees assume a command rather than an advisory attitude, then agency leadership has failed. If the committee's only assignment is to render advice on specific rule or policy proposals, this supervisory tendency is negated if the committee is given temporary status.

It has been claimed that important interests may be devoid of representation on advisory committees—that only vocal and well-organ-

---

[3] The literature concerning public participation in administration is well developed. One widely held opinion is that in practically all cases the public interest will be successfully guarded and realized only if full participation by affected interests is permitted, encouraged, and fostered. See for example, O. B. Conaway, Jr. (ed.), *Democracy in Federal Administration* (Washington, D. C.: U. S. Department of Agriculture Graduate School, 1955); U. S. Department of Agriculture Graduate School, *Lectures on Administrative Regulation* (Washington, D. C., 1945); Walter Gellhorn, *Federal Administrative Proceedings* (Baltimore: Johns Hopkins University Press, 1941); and Ordway Tead, *New Adventures in Democracy: Practical Applications of the Democratic Idea* (New York: McGraw Hill Book Co., Inc., 1939) Still other writings are much more cautious about public participation, emphasizing the frequent disparities between public and private interests as manifested in public administration. See, for example, the works cited in note 1, page 69. President Kennedy apparently feared participative devices might diffuse administrative responsibility I order to 'clarify and pinpoint executive responsibility," he abolished fifty-eight government committees, including a number of advisory committees, during March and April 196 See the *New York Times*, March 12, 1961, and April 9, 1961.

ized interests gain representation, while poorly financed or unorganized groups are left unrepresented. It is true that the advisory committee technique works most effectively when the various interests involved are readily distinguishable and well organized, and gain representation on the committee. A resourceful administrator, however, overrides the disadvantages of unrepresented interests by supplementing the advisory committee technique with other participation devices: He holds informal conferences or consultations with otherwise unrepresented but interested persons or groups; he schedules public hearings, with adequate notice given to all interests that are likely to be affected; or he appoints to the committee members who are to serve as public representatives.

A related charge is that administrators often "load" committees with persons of one viewpoint. This happens only when there is a failure of administrative leadership. If an administrator actually follows this practice, he inevitably incurs the enmity of groups whose views are not represented on the committee and thereby defeats his agency objectives.

Another criticism consists of the claim that capable and interested persons often cannot be found to serve on such committees. This problem frequently arises when the qualifications of committee members are prescribed too narrowly by statute. The fault here is that of the legislature rather than of the committee technique itself. The appropriate remedy is corrective legislation.

Still another criticism is the assertion that the representative advisory committee operates as a bargaining process rather than as a search for truth. The counter argument to this complaint is that successful public policy making in a heterogeneous and democratic society requires compromise and, hence, bargaining.

Finally, the complaint has been made that advisory committees generally meet in secret, behind closed doors.[4] When an agency makes

[4] "In recent months, I have been much concerned about the secrecy that surrounds the legislative functions exercised by advisory committees of various kinds. A great many policies of government are being influenced, if not actually formed and framed, by advisory committees of many kinds. They are formulating policies upon which the fortunes of millions of citizens depend. Often no voice of the

it a practice to hold public hearings with prior notice on controversial policy proposals, charges that its proceedings are secret become infrequent. Some agencies often open their advisory committee proceedings to the public when controversial policy proposals are considered, though formal public hearings on such proposals may later be held.

Positive Human Relations

There are students of public administration, this writer among them, who defend advisory committees as a device for enhancing democratic administration.[5] They base their argument upon the general theory that the governed should have the opportunity to participate in their government—in the administrative part as well as in the legislative part—and that the advisory committee represents one device for such participation.

Defenders of advisory committees also rely upon practical considerations. They assert that the advisory committee and other participation devices provide a valuable source of factual information and opinions for sound agency action.

Defenders of advisory committees allege that such committees clarify issues and thereby shorten public hearings that may be held subsequently. They claim that an understanding may develop between administrators and affected parties at advisory committee discussions that serves to facilitate subsequent administration of agency policies or rules. It is also suggested that advisory committee deliberations serve as a test for the reasonableness of proposed agency

---

public is heard. There is no public examination of witnesses. There is no public debate of alternative courses of action. A secrecy that never would be tolerated in the legislative branch of government enshrouds the entire operation. . . . We need to make certain that . . . we have not substituted relatively anonymous, semi-private, secret rule-making agencies for open legislative methods in the development of national policy" (James R. Wiggins, "Government Communications with the Public," in O. B. Conaway, Jr. [ed.], *op. cit.*, pp. 54-64, at p. 62).

[5] See the relevant works cited in note 3, page 71. See also Julius E. Eitington, "The Committee Revisited," *Personnel Administration*, XXIII (November-December 1960), 10-18; and Frank C. Moore, *Greater Citizen Participation in Government* (Pittsburgh: Institute of Local Government, University of Pittsburgh, 1957).

policies or rules. Another argument contends that the formalized representation of various groups afforded by advisory committees renders greater assurance to those groups that their interests and opinions will be made known to and considered by the administrators, thus facilitating subsequent administration of agency policies. This acceptance, it is reasoned, is fostered by the fact that advisory committees generally comprise persons of considerable prestige in their groups and communities.

Finally, it is asserted that the advisory committee affords a more systematic means of obtaining facts and opinion than the informal conference or consultation technique, and that it is a less expensive device than the public hearing.[6]

Whether the rationale relates to a theory of democracy, informed administrative action, or an educational or public relations function, it apparently derives from some social theory that emphasizes positive and effective human relations in groups and thus contrasts sharply with the "struggle for power" theory of the detractors of advisory committees.

Administrative Leadership

After all has been said for and against advisory committees, they are an inexpensive means of gaining important information upon which workable and responsible administrative action can be based.[7]

The advisory committee, moreover, serves as a public relations device for the skilled administrator. Though an administrator may

[6] Committee members usually serve without pay, although they often have many years of experience in their respective fields. Whether advisory committee members are compensated for their services usually depends upon the sacrifice they must make. Oftentimes, the opportunity to participate in policy formulation is compensation enough, especially if a member's private interests are allied with the committee's work. Service without compensation, moreover, may mean that the persons who serve have motives higher than expectancy of pecuniary gain.

[7] For British experience, see W. J. M. MacKenzie, "Committees in Administration," *Public Administration*, XXXI (Autumn 1953), 235-44; and "Committee Procedure," *Public Administration*, XXXVI (Autumn 1958), 249-59, a reproduction of a booklet prepared within the Treasury for official use "as a guide on general points of procedure for the civil servant who is appointed secretary to a committee, and as an *aide-memoire* for civil servants who act as chairmen of committees."

feel that the information-supplying function alone does not justify an advisory committee, there are two situations in which use of the technique is desirable in terms of public relations. One such situation exists when the agency is considering a set of proposed rules or policies that financially burden or restrict affected persons. Another exists when two or more interests are likely to be directly affected by proposed agency action.

It is axiomatic that a policy is potentially more controversial when it actually restricts or regulates than when it merely prescribes procedures or facilitates the rendering of services or benefits. In terms of public relations, however, it is not quite so necessary to create an advisory committee when only one organized group declares its interest in a proposed policy. The executive committee of such a group, through informal conference or consultation with the agency, usually acts in an advisory capacity without formal organization. This is a common situation confronting most professional examining and licensing agencies; generally, a single organized group evinces interest in proposed administrative action.

Administrative discretion concerning the character and use of advisory committees is sometimes restricted by legislative interference. Because the circumstances confronting an administrator constantly change, he normally wants the right to determine when an advisory committee may serve a desirable administrative purpose.[8] Likewise, he wants freedom to determine the membership of committees, because the success or failure of a committee often depends on the qualities of its members. Yet the administrator usually seeks to preclude the accusation that he has "loaded" a committee.[9] One work-

[8] An extreme example of legislative interference in Wisconsin is a specific statutory requirement that a so-called "advisory committee" have final "review" authority over policy decisions of the commissioner of the state Savings and Loan Department (Wis. Stat., sec. 215.60 [1957]). Wisconsin's revised Administrative Procedure Act encourages the use of advisory committees by authorizing each agency, at its discretion, "to appoint committees of experts or interested persons or representatives of the general public to advise it with respect to any contemplated rule making." But the act stipulates that "the powers of such committees shall be advisory only" (Wis. Stat., sec. 227.018 [1955]).

[9] As a practical matter, no constitutional difficulties are apparent with respect

able method of avoiding such charges is for him to choose members from among a number of nominees submitted by each interest group to be represented on the committee. The actual number of interests to be represented on the committee then governs its size. But the skilled administrator is mindful that the larger a committee becomes, the more unwieldy it is likely to be.

The advisory committee technique is more effective with respect to the large policy-making project—the formulation or revision of complete codes or standards, for example—than for the minor amendment of rules. It follows, then, that most committees whose sole function is to advise on policy making have temporary rather than permanent status. The longer a committee functions, the greater the possibility that its members may either lose interest in their purpose or develop a supervisory as against an advisory attitude. The skilled administrator never forgets that he—not the advisory committee—is responsible for the form and content of agency policy.

It is common practice for one of the agency's officers to serve as a member of the committee. Frequently, the agency representative acts as secretary or chairman. Such a person often prepares the agenda for committee meetings and arranges for staff services when needed. He provides necessary leadership in the committee and acts as a liaison between it and the agency. What is perhaps more important, he also does the initial drafting of policies considered by the committee, a task that is not feasible for large committees.[10]

---

to advisory committees, especially if their functions are purely advisory. Since constitutional due process usually does not require public participation in connection with most rule-making proceedings, it would seem that in those instances the courts would not concern themselves with the fairness of the composition or procedure of any advisory committee that may have been created. In one of the few instances in which the issue of unfairness of the composition and procedure of an advisory committee was presented to the United States Supreme Court, the Court had no difficulty in finding that statutory procedures had been complied with, and gave little attention to the constitutional issues raised (Opp Cotton Mills v. Administrator of the Wage and Hour Division of the Department of Labor, 312 U. S. 126 [1941]).

[10] See E. H. Simpson, *The Mechanics of Committee Work: An Essay on the Tasks of a Committee Secretary* (Brussels: International Institute of Administrative Sciences, 1952).

PUBLIC HEARINGS

The use of public hearings in policy making as a public participation technique likewise has disadvantages as well as advantages.

Advantages and Disadvantages

Some of the *advantages* of the public hearing as a part of the administrative policy-making process are:

1. The public hearing gives members of the unorganized general public an opportunity to make their views known to the administrator. Such persons are likely to be left out of informal conferences or advisory committees, and the public hearing is usually the only procedural means by which they may participate in agency policy making, the only reliable device by which they can be given the opportunity to be heard prior to the adoption of a policy. The hearing shifts the decision concerning who shall participate from the agency to each affected or interested individual. It therefore maximizes individual choice to participate.

2. In some instances the public hearing may be the only feasible means by which the administrator can obtain necessary facts and views. For example, when interests are geographically dispersed throughout an agency's territorial jurisdiction, hearings on the same proposal may be held at various convenient places to maximize participation and to avoid difficulties of travel which conferences or committee meetings might entail for participants.

3. The public hearing often has a measure of educational value for generating public opinion with respect to a proposed policy.

4. A public hearing lessens the danger that an administrator who is sensitive to interest group demands will adopt policies responsive to the views of organized and articulate groups at the expense of less well organized and less articulate groups.

5. Finally, a public hearing makes it less likely that the substance of a policy will be politically inexpedient. In a sense, a public hearing may be viewed as a test of the reasonableness, political feasibility, timing, and acceptability of a proposed policy.

Some *disadvantages* or limitations of the public hearing technique are:

1. An administrator who decides to hold a public hearing prior to the promulgation of a policy must be willing to pay the price of delay in putting the policy into effect. Such delay may be highly undesirable in circumstances requiring quick policy action.

2. Hearings cost money, especially if testimony is fully recorded and transcribed. They also require time and effort on the part of administrators, which sometimes might be put to better use.

3. Many people are reluctant to speak in a public forum, whether out of shyness or because they wish to avoid publicity. Accordingly, despite the holding of hearings, important facts and opinions may remain unknown to administrators. This limitation of the public hearing technique can be surmounted in part by supplementing the hearing with written questionnaires or by holding informal conferences after the hearing.

4. Holding a public hearing provides no assurance that interested persons who are not organized and who live at considerable distances from the place of the hearing will attend. This limitation can be partially overcome by holding hearings in various areas of the governmental jurisdiction. However, costs will increase, and more delay will be encountered, in these instances.

5. Many participants speak at great length and present irrelevant and unreliable material. Firmness and tact on the part of the presiding officer can minimize irrelevancies, whereas the use of effective procedures can minimize presentation of undesirable material.

To sum up: The administrator does not evaluate the public hearing solely in terms of the number and diversity of the persons who attend. His decision to hold a hearing is tantamount to extension of the right of participation to *any* affected person. The administrator must decide whether the advantages override the apparent disadvantages of public hearings. If he decides not to hold hearings, is he not still accountable for his actions to his superiors, to the legislature, to the courts, and through them to the public he serves? Is he not still subject to many checks—audit, budget, formal, and informal—within the framework of limited government? Above all, he knows that his policy decisions cannot persist interminably if they contravene the higher law of the legislature or the still higher law of the Constitution.

It is questionable whether many administrators reflect in such theoretical terms when deciding whether to hold a hearing. Public administrators normally think more pragmatically. They are conscious of such factors as time and money, and they know that the public hearing involves delay and expenditures. For these practical reasons, the public hearing has not been used as extensively in agency policy making as its advantages would warrant.

Due Process

Assuming that the administrative agencies of a governmental jurisdiction are not required by the legislature to hold public hearings in their policy making, the question remains whether constitutional considerations of due process or equity require such hearings. It is often stated that a public hearing is not a prerequisite to due process when the nature of the administrative action is quasi-legislative rather than quasi-judicial. Court cases on the subject are numerous, and the writers who have analyzed them agree that the terms "quasi-legislative" and "quasi-judicial" are mere labels to justify or rationalize conclusions reached on other grounds.[11] Some of these other grounds are:

1. *The number of persons affected by the administrative action.* If the persons regulated or otherwise affected are few in number, the proceeding takes on more of the aspects of a court proceeding, and notice and hearing are more likely to be necessary to satisfy due process requirements than where the action affects a large class of persons.

[11] See, for example, Morris Duane, "Mandatory Hearings in the Rule Making Process," *Annals of the American Academy of Political and Social Science,* CCXXI (1943), 115-22; and Davis, *Administrative Law and Government,* Chapter 7.

One writer has stated that the controlling criterion is not the number of persons affected but whether the controversy relates to facts concerning particular persons.[12]

2. *The directness of the effect of the administrative action upon those affected.* If the effect is direct and substantial, either personal or economic, notice and hearing are more likely to be prerequisites to due process than if the effect of the policy is indirect and incidental.

3. *The need for immediate administrative action in the public interest.* In cases of emergency, the courts are more likely to be sympathetic toward dispensing with notice and hearing than otherwise.

4. *The presence or absence of legally recognizable interest.* No notice or hearing is required if the interest affected is not a legally recognizable or discernible one, but the concept "legally recognizable interest" is itself a changing one.

5. *The availability of a hearing at a later stage of the proceeding.* If a full administrative or judicial hearing is available at some stage of the proceeding before agency action becomes final, that generally is considered sufficient.

Given so many variables, it would seem that the most that can be said is that constitutional due process considerations generally do not require any public hearing in the administrative policy-making process, but that hearings are usually required in matters involving price control, wage control, and rate fixing whether because of the economic stakes or because of antagonisms involved. It is questionable whether due process so universally requires public hearings in any category of policy-making proceedings that a legislature will, on constitutional grounds alone, require hearings in a general administrative procedure act.

Legislative Requirement

Though public hearings are generally not necessary to satisfy constitutional due process requirements, the legislature can decide to require them as part of the agency policy process. For a number of

[12] Davis, *Administrative Law* (1951), p. 258.

reasons, legislators are more inclined than administrators to hold to a presumption in favor of public hearings in administrative policy making. After all, their "regularized" procedures of lawmaking involve public hearings. Why, then, they reason, should not administrators likewise hold hearings when they legislate—when they make policies having the force and effect of law?

This logic would appear unassailable to legislators were there no apparent disadvantages to public hearings. Despite their general disposition toward the holding of public hearings, even legislators recognize that there are situations in which hearings are impractical. Consequently, they have the problem of determining those situations in which public hearings should not be required.

Exceptions. This is not an easy problem to solve. Legislatures that have dealt with it vary greatly in the exceptions they permit. Kentucky requires hearings where practicable,[13] while Minnesota exempts from its hearing requirement only rule making by certain professional and regulatory examining and licensing boards and rule making related to the management, discipline, and release of persons committed to state institutions.[14] Both the federal government and Nebraska have general notice and hearing requirements, but they are almost as flexible as the Kentucky statute. The Federal Administrative Procedure Act provides that no hearing need be held if the agency finds that notice and public hearing procedure in specific instances of rule making is unnecessary, impracticable, or contrary to the public interest.[15] Under the Nebraska act, the governor may waive the hearing requirement merely for cause shown.[16]

Six states—Arizona, California, Michigan, Ohio, Virginia, and Wisconsin—exempt emergency situations from public hearings.[17] Doubtless, there are instances in which an agency must act with dis-

13 Ky. Stat., sec. 13.125 (1952).
14 Minn. Stat., sec. 15.042 (4) and 15.044 (1949).
15 5 U. S. C. A. 1003 (a) (1950).
16 Neb. Laws, ch. 359, sec. 1 (1953).
17 Ariz. Laws, ch. 97, sec. 8 (1952); 1951 Calif. Gov't. Code and 1953 Supp., sec. 11421 (b); Mich. Comp. Laws (1948), Mich. Acts. ch. 103, sec. 24.101 (2), 319.16, 319.72 (1953); Ohio Code Ann., sec. 154-64 (f) (Page, 1946); Va. Code Ann., sec. 9-6.5 (1952 Supp.); Wis. Stat., sec. 227.02 (1) (c), 227.027 (1) (1955).

patch, and the requirements of expediency outweigh inequities that might arise from lack of notice and hearing on a proposed agency policy action. Unless reasonably circumscribed, however, the emergency exemption provision tends to be abused by many agencies. For example, a California legislative committee found that many state agencies did not even make a pretense of having the facts to substantiate the existence of emergencies when they adopted emergency regulations.[18] To obviate abuse of the privilege that permits agencies to forego hearings in emergency situations, Wisconsin stipulates that a rule adopted pursuant to emergency procedures is effective for a period of only 120 days.[19] This gives an agency ample time to adopt a rule in accordance with regular policy-making procedures if a permanent policy is found to be needed.

Almost all general administrative procedure acts exempt policy making related to internal agency management from general notice and hearing requirements, presumably because such proceedings are of little concern to the general public.[20] The federal, Indiana, Virginia, and Wisconsin acts exempt policy making with respect to military affairs. Indiana exempts agency proceedings concerned with public higher education, while Virginia and Wisconsin exempt those related to public education in general. Virginia ambiguously exempts "mere instructions," as well as rule making related to the receipt of public assistance.[21]

18 "Some agencies make a pro forma finding of facts which on their face clearly show that there is no emergency in any sense of the word, but that the agency is merely using the emergency process in the interest of saving time and effort, plus a nominal sum for advertising and holding public hearings. It is found that generally, the agencies which deal with the regulation and licensing of businesses and professions are among the most frequent users, and abusers, of the emergency processes . . ." (Senate Interim Committee on Administrative Regulations, *Second Preliminary and Partial Report* [California Senate: Senate Interim Committee, 1953], p. 11; see also *ibid.*, pp. 48, 77, 80-82).

19 Wis. Stat., sec. 227.027 (1) (1955).

20 5 U. S. C. A. 1003 (a) (1950); Ariz. Laws, ch. 97, sec. 8 (1952); Ind. Stat. Ann., sec. 60-1504 (Burns, 1951); Iowa Code Ann., sec. 17A.1(3) (Supp. 1953); Mich. Comp. Laws (1948), Mich. Acts, ch. 197 (1952), Mich. Acts, ch. 103, sec. 24.101 (2) (1953); Minn. Stat., sec. 15.0444 (1949); Va. Code Ann., sec. 9-6.2 (b) (1952 Supp.).

21 See, for example, Va. Code Ann., sec. 9-6.2 (d) (1952 Supp.); 5 U. S. C. A. 1003 (1) (1950); Ind. Stat. Ann., sec. 60-1504 (Burns, 1951); Wis. Stat., sec. 227.01 (5) (f) and (i) (1955).

Though public hearings are usually considered important in the fixing of rates, prices, or tariffs, California exempts such policy making.[22] Moreover, several states exempt policy making involving public utilities, workmen's compensation, unemployment compensation, and taxation, apparently because special procedures are otherwise required and should be controlling rather than any generally applicable procedures.

Like Minnesota, Wisconsin exempts policy making concerned with the management, discipline, and release of persons committed to state institutions.[23] Wisconsin also exempts policy making related to highway construction, maintenance, and relocation; the use of public libraries; state and local government personnel management; and water level determinations, among other matters.[24] California, Virginia, and Wisconsin exempt rule making on the use of highways when a regulation is made known to the public by means of signs or signals.[25]

Only Wisconsin seems to have incorporated another category of exemptions from the general hearing requirement: minor policy changes where little or no discretion is vested in an agency, such as a modification to conform to a statute that has been changed or enacted after the adoption of an agency policy; or a change in the language of an existing agency policy to conform to a controlling judicial decision or to comply with a federal requirement.[26]

Presumption in favor.   Though there is a great number of policy-making situations in which a public hearing is not practicable, and certain exceptions are permitted, this does not prevent legislatures from favoring a general presumption that an agency should hold a public hearing prior to adopting, amending, or repealing a policy. Such a procedure, many legislators believe, accords with traditional democratic concepts. It also permits bringing to the attention

---

22 1951 Calif. Gov't. Code and 1953 Supp., sec. 11421 (a) (1).
23 Minn. Stat., sec. 15.044 (1949); Wis. Stat., sec. 227.01 (1955).
24 Wis. Stat., sec. 227.01 (5) (1955).
25 *Ibid.*; 1951 Calif. Gov't. Code and 1953 Supp., sec. 11421 (2); Va. Code Ann., 9-6.2 (b) (1952 Supp.).
26 Wis. Stat., sec. 227.02 (1) (b) (1955).

of administrators facts and opinions of which they might not otherwise be cognizant, thereby reducing the possibility of agency policies
that are objectionable to the legislature or the general public. Conversely, it is reasoned that the hearing procedure affords agencies an
opportunity to educate interested persons concerning the need for
proposed policies.

The question still confronts a legislature whether to remove all
discretion from administrators by requiring them to hold hearings
in every policy-making instance not explicitly exempted.

The answer surely would have to be affirmative if it were possible
for a legislature to foresee and enumerate in its controlling legislation
all situations in which a public hearing would not serve any good
purpose. But, unfortunately, no legislature possesses such omnis-
cience. Moreover, for a legislature entirely to remove such procedural
flexibility in the attainment of agency goals is to move toward elimi-
nating the very *raison d'être* of public administration. The prime
reason for a legislature to resort to the administrative process in the
first instance is to achieve that kind of governmental flexibility which
legislatures themselves cannot achieve.

On the hearing question—as with so many questions of legislative
control of the administrative process—the basic issue becomes what
a legislature can reasonably require of administrators without unduly
fettering their discretion. The Wisconsin legislature believes that it
has worked out an effective solution to this problem. Not only may
a Wisconsin agency forego holding a hearing in any of the several
exempted situations, as noted earlier, but in all other instances an
agency is permitted to publish notice of its intention to adopt a specified rule proposal without hearing unless the agency receives a subsequent petition requesting a hearing that is signed by a certain
number of interested persons.[27]

In the absence of constitutional or legislative requirements that
hearings be held, many administrators hold them whenever they believe that a hearing will serve their objectives. Many factors condi-

[27] Wis. Stat., sec. 227.02 (1) (e) (1955).

tion this decision. But, increasingly, doubt is resolved in favor of using the hearing technique.

Notice of Hearings

An important characteristic of a public hearing is advance public notice. Most jurisdictions that have adopted general procedure legislation dealing with hearings have required some kind of notice. The pertinent provisions usually deal with three questions: When must notice be given? How and to whom must it be given? What must the notice contain?

Time. For notice to be effective, it is elementary that it be given prior to the hearing. The Arizona and California acts merely provide that notice must be given "prior to the adoption" of any rule,[28] and the Michigan and federal acts make no reference to a specific time for giving notice. Requirements of other jurisdictions range from thirty days to at least four days prior to the hearing. The Virginia act provides that notice must be published not less than fifteen nor more than thirty days prior to a hearing date.[29]

The convenience of the affected public is often the controlling consideration. Notice is given far enough in advance of a hearing date to give interested persons ample opportunity to attend the hearing, yet not so far in advance that they may forget to attend. Whatever general notice requirements a legislature decides to impose on administrative establishments, some administrative discretion is usually allowed. If the agency policy proposals to be considered at a hearing are voluminous, the period between the notice and hearing is often extended to enable interested persons to study drafts of the proposals. Appropriately, therefore, a legislature merely fixes the minimum time prior to a hearing before which an agency must give notice, and thus permits the agency to decide whether to give notice further in advance of the minimum time. In most instances,

28 Ariz. Laws, ch. 97, sec. 7 (1952); 1951 Calif. Gov't. Code and 1953 Supp., sec. 11423.
29 Va. Code Ann., sec. 9-6.4 (1952 Supp.).

ten to fifteen days' notice is regarded as a sufficient legislative requirement. Where a periodic supplement to an administrative code
is designated by the legislature as the required place for giving official notice of hearings, the supplement's publication schedule has a
bearing on the time of notice.

Manner.   Publication in a newspaper of general circulation is the
most common manner of giving notice of hearing that is imposed by
legislatures. California, Michigan, and Minnesota require that notice
be mailed to all persons who have filed such a request with agencies.[30]
Ohio requires that each agency determine by rule how notice of
hearings shall be given.[31] If the most effective means of giving notice
is sought by an agency, then it ought to have some discretion to tailor
the means to fit each hearing occasion as it arises. It is widely held,
however, that minimum notice requirements prescribed by a legislature, if reasonable, do not unduly constrict such administrative
discretion.

Notice by mailing on an agency's own initiative is adequate only
when the agency's clientele is known with certainty and is relatively
small. Otherwise, interested persons are ignored, and the cost of mailing may be excessive. In order to preclude both omissions and excessive costs, some agencies require that persons desiring notice of
all hearings in a particular field of administrative activity file their
names and addresses with the agencies and pay a subscription fee
to defray the costs of mailing. The Wisconsin act requires publication in the notice section of its administrative register and the trans-
mission of notice to any member of the legislature who has filed a
request with the revisor of statutes.[32]

Content.   With respect to the content of notice, the Arizona and
Wisconsin acts are typical. They require that notice include the time,
place, and nature of the proceedings, reference to the statutory
authority pursuant to which the agency proposes to adopt the rule,

[30] 1951 Calif. Gov't. Code and 1953 Supp., sec. 11432 (b); Mich. Comp. Laws
(1948), Mich. Acts, ch. 197 (1952), Mich. Acts, ch. 103, sec. 24.102 (3) (1953); Minn.
Stat., sec. 15.042 (4) (1949).

[31] Ohio Code Ann., secs. 154-64 (a) (Page, 1946).

[32] Wis. Stat., sec. 227.021 (1) (a) and (b) (1955).

either the express terms or an informative summary or description of the policy proposal, and such other matters as otherwise may be prescribed by statute applicable to the agency concerned.[33] Verbatim reproduction of the proposal is not always practical, especially if it is lengthy. Moreover, since an "agency" by definition is an organ of government that has authority to adopt generally applicable policies or rules,[34] the requirement that express statutory authority for a rule be included might appear superfluous. But an agency may have general authority to adopt rules without having authority to adopt rules in specific areas or of specific kinds. At any rate, these requirements do not impose any hardships upon administrative agencies.

Hearing Procedures

Most state legislatures do not prescribe the manner in which hearings shall be conducted. Determination of hearing procedures is generally within agency discretion. A typical statutory provision requires agencies to afford interested persons an opportunity to present statements, arguments, or contentions in writing, with or without the opportunity to present the same orally. A few states require that each agency consider all relevant matter presented to it before adopting a rule. In addition, a few states authorize agencies to administer oaths and to adjourn hearings from time to time. The Ohio act requires a stenographic record of hearing proceedings and authorizes agencies to pass on the admissibility of evidence.[35] The federal act prescribes detailed procedures for cases where "rules are required by statute to be made on the record after opportunity for an agency hearing," as distinguished from cases where no such requirement is made.[36]

When framing general procedural legislation, a legislature may consider whether to prescribe by statute a single set of procedural

33 Ariz. Laws, ch. 97, sec. 7 (1952); Wis. Stat., sec. 227.021 (3) (1955).

34 "An administrative agency is a governmental authority, other than a court and other than a legislative body, which affects rights of private parties through either adjudication or rule making" (Davis, *Administrative Law and Government* [1960], p. 11).

35 Ohio Code Ann., sec. 154-164 (c) (2) and (4) (Page, 1946).

36 5 U. S. C. A. 1003 (b) (1950).

requirements for all administrative hearings. It should not do this if it wishes to refrain from jeopardizing necessary administrative flexibility. And any attempt by a legislature to judicialize the hearing process compresses the situational exercise of administrative discretion. When a proposed policy prompts sharp alignments of opposing factions, or otherwise creates a contentious or controversial atmosphere, administrators tend to introduce judicial features into the hearing proceeding. But they prefer that this should be an administrative decision free from the intrusion of general procedural legislation.

Though an administrative agency is not required to act in the manner of a court when it is making policies, there are still questions of hearing procedure for an administrator to consider.

Who presides at hearings? The ability of the person who presides at a hearing determines to a great extent the quality of the hearing. Not only is an able chairman familiar with hearing procedures and techniques, but he is familiar also with the subject matter under consideration. Because substantive knowledge of a policy proposal, together with its administrative implications, is usually more important in a policy hearing than procedural knowledge, it is generally not the practice to draw the presiding officer from a central pool of hearing masters or officers, as some jurisdictions do for adjudicative hearings. Accordingly, if the head of an agency cannot preside, a high-ranking officer does so, or, failing this, a person high in authority is at least present at the hearing. This practice also assures persons in attendance that their views are made known to the ultimate policy-making authority of the agency.

How does the hearing begin? Regardless of the fact that notice of the hearing presumably has apprised interested persons at least generally of its nature and purpose, the beginning of the hearing is usually given over to a summary of the results of the agency's experience and investigation that have formed the basis for or given rise to the need for the policy proposal. Not only are agency reasons for a new policy made known, and hence irrational objections obviated, but interested persons are presented with a fair opportunity to refute facts or opinions offered by the agency in support of the proposal.

Are witnesses sworn?   Whether witnesses are sworn is properly a question for administrative judgment in each hearing situation. The mere presentation of views or arguments concerning a proposed agency policy normally does not require placing a participant under oath. However, if the hearing is contentious or litigious in nature, or if persons appearing tend to present exaggerated, irresponsible, or irrelevant opinions and arguments, placing witnesses under oath tends to make a psychological contribution to the efficiency of the hearing.

Do rules of evidence apply?   Most writers on administrative law agree that rules of evidence are not required in policy-making hearings. The able presiding officer nevertheless attempts to keep participation relevant to the proposal under consideration.

Is oral presentation restricted?   As stated before, most general procedure statutes dealing with hearings require that interested persons be given the opportunity to present written facts and arguments, with or without the opportunity to present the same orally. (Regardless of such requirements, it is difficult to conceive of any circumstance that would prevent any agency from willingly receiving written materials.) It is doubtful that "hearings" may consist solely of the presentation of written material. But oral presentations are usually limited when they are considered likely to prolong a hearing unduly.

What kind of record is kept?   Again, the question of what kind of record of hearing proceedings is made is generally a matter for administrative judgment. Though some sort of record usually is kept, verbatim stenographic recording and transcription are unnecessary in many hearings. Cost is an important factor, and the decision is situational.

It is evident that most policy-making hearings are informal as compared with adjudicative or judicial hearings. Circumstances may commend occasional resort to courtlike proceedings, but their feasibility is properly a matter for administrative decision on a hearing-by-hearing basis.

OTHER PARTICIPATION DEVICES

No device for public participation in administrative policy making is utilized nearly so much as the three most prominent techniques: informal conferences and consultation; advisory committees; and public hearings. However, in addition to these, some jurisdictions have employed a number of means of effecting public participation in agency policy making. Interest representation through appointment, resort to boards and commissions, and research and development contracts—all discussed in the previous chapter—afford participative opportunities for outside interests to advise on agency policy proposals as well as to initiate policy ideas. Another participative device remaining to be discussed is the use of petitions.

Most general administrative procedure acts provide that any interested person may petition an agency for the adoption, amendment, or repeal of any rule. Some further provide that each agency shall prescribe the form for such petitions and the procedure for their submission, consideration, and disposition.[37] The Iowa and Michigan acts require the agency to call a public hearing on the petition, but Iowa stipulates that at least twenty substantially interested persons must have signed the petition.[38] The California and federal acts require that the agency either call a hearing on the petition or deny the petition in writing.[39] Under the other acts, an agency is not required to do anything upon receipt of a petition.

As observed in Chapter 1, most policy making in public administration is initiated by variable and informal means. By comparison, formal petitions for initiating policies are seldom received by administrative agencies. Moreover, the right of an individual to petition his government doubtless exists without any statutory authorization. Though perhaps superfluous, a provision sanctioning petitions

[37] See, e.g., Wis. Stat., sec. 227.015 (1955).

[38] Iowa Code Ann., sec. 17A.6 (Supplement 1953); Mich. Acts, ch. 103, sec. 24.103 (1953).

[39] 1951 Calif. Gov't. Code and 1953 Supp., sec. 11427; 5 U. S. C. A. 1003 (d) and 1005 (d) (1950).

for agency policy making is not undesirable. But if a legislature so provides, it should also prescribe the procedure for submission and require that the agency inform the petitioner of its action. Unless petitions evoke some form of agency action, either affirmative or negative, they prove valueless.

Another device, as observed in Chapter 1, is delegation to private groups, in fact if not in theory, of authority to draft agency policies by virtue of the practice known as incorporation by reference. This occurs most frequently in highly technical and professional fields of administrative activity.

Yet another participation technique is that of providing a delay in the effective date following promulgation of an agency policy, thus permitting an interested person to request revision before the policy goes into effect.

Some combination of the public participation devices discussed in this chapter generally assures the opportunity for public participation in agency policy making.

PART TWO
***
PROBLEMS
OF
POLICY CONTROL

Chapter Four

✳✳✳

The Right
to Know

It may appear almost trite to suggest that members of the public who are affected by agency policies have a right to know of what such policies consist; or, to put the matter more simply, that those affected by law have a right to know what the law is. Nevertheless, the lack of adequate publicity of administrative policies is one of the most serious defects of the administrative process. The problem is not a new one. The story is told of Caligula, the Roman emperor, who caused great hardship for his subjects by refusing to publish the laws, that when finally he did consent to do so, he used such fine print and posted them at such a height that the people found them extremely difficult to read.[1]

---

[1] One of the earliest recorded British instances of delegation was the Statute of Proclamations of 1539, which delegated broad powers to Henry VIII to set forth proclamations. Included was a clause which prescribed that every sheriff or other officer to whom the king's proclamations were directed should, within fourteen days, proclaim them in market towns, other towns, or villages and post them up "openly and upon places convenient" therein. See Cecil T. Carr, "Delegated Legislation," in J. Forrester Davison and Nathan D. Grundstein, *Cases and Readings on Administrative Law* (Indianapolis: The Bobbs-Merrill Company, Inc., 1952), pp. 760-62, at p. 761.

HIDDEN LAW

Whether because of political considerations, including the desire to mute criticism and minimize opposition, or perhaps, more importantly, because of the press of other business, administrative agencies often do not publish their policies in any form convenient to those affected by them. Some administrators carry policies in their heads, and they become known only when occasion elicits them through correspondence or a telephone conversation. One state administrator wrote a prospective applicant that it was against the policy of his agency to license *part-time* automobile salesmen. Yet no statutory authority existed for this policy, nor was it published in any form. When asked about this, he replied that he wanted to protect the public against "fly-by-night operators."[2] As in many such instances, the problem is not the relation of the agency-made law to the public interest, but rather the right of the citizen to have knowledge of the law and his rights and obligations under it. If he cannot easily discover agency law, then his rights and interests are bound to be adversely affected. Time, money, and opportunity may be lost to him.

Often, the client of a public agency must probe deeply into fugitive agency sources to discover what the agency requires of him. Generally applicable policies that directly affect private rights and interests are frequently discoverable only in internal agency communications such as staff manuals, memoranda, reports, or interoffice circulars. Such policies are hidden law. In 1941, the federal Attorney General's Committee on Administrative Procedure observed:

> To all but a few specialists, such a situation leads to a feeling of frustration. Laymen and lawyers alike, accustomed to the traditional processes of legislation and adjudication, are baffled by a lack of published information to which they can turn when confronted with an administrative problem.
>
> Such a state of affairs will at least partially explain a number of types of criticisms of the administrative process. Where necessary information

[2] Wisconsin Legislative Council, *Interim Report II on Administrative Rule Making*, p. 82.

must be secured through oral discussion or inquiry, it is natural that parties should complain of a "government of men." Where public regulation is not adequately expressed in rules, complaints regarding "unrestrained delegation of legislative authority" are aggravated. Where the process of decision is not clearly outlined, charges of "star-chamber proceedings" may be anticipated.[3]

A basic problem, then, is the failure of government to make agency law known to its citizens when it is obligated to do so. And this is a problem fraught with fundamental considerations involving the essence of equitable and democratic government.

It is not surprising, therefore, that this basic problem has received increasing attention on both the federal and state levels of government. The most persistent purpose of state general administrative procedure acts has been to provide adequate publicity for administrative policies. More than half the states have general administrative procedure acts dealing with this matter. In 1933, by presidential action, provision was first made for the publication of federal administrative regulations "in the manner of other laws." As a result, the *Federal Register* comprises the daily publication of new "rules, regulations, and orders" having "general applicability and legal effect."[4] Much has been accomplished since the 1930's to improve the publicity afforded administrative policies.[5] The question is no longer whether to publish, but rather the practical one of what and how to publish.[6]

SYSTEMS OF PUBLICATION

Prior to general administrative procedure legislation on the state level, and the *Federal Register* system on the national level, either

---

[3] Committee on Administrative Procedure, *Final Report of the Attorney General's Committee on Administrative Procedure*, p. 25.

[4] *Ibid.*, pp. 25-26; Federal Register Act, 44 U. S. C. A. 305 (a) (1953 Supplement).

[5] See, for example, Federal Administrative Procedure Act, 60 U. S. Stat. 237 (1946), 5 U. S. C. A. 1001 *et seq.*

[6] For discussion of the congressional problems in this respect, see Francis E. Rourke, "Administrative Secrecy: A Congressional Dilemma," *American Political Science Review*, LIV (September 1960), 684-94.

administrative agencies published their own policies or the policies remained unpublished. Usually, publication was a matter for administrative discretion, but occasionally a statute would require an agency to publish all its policies or specific kinds of policies.

Most administrative procedure acts have attempted to systematize the publication of policies. They define the generic term "rule" and then require that any nonexempt agency policy within the definition be published as a rule. The systems vary, but certain general distinctions can be made.

Requisites. The primary requisites of a publication system are economy, flexibility, reliability, and convenience, the relative value of each being a matter of judgment. Cost is always an important, and frequently the deciding, factor in determining adoption of one system as against another. An effective system is sufficiently flexible so as not to hamper an agency unduly in changing its rules. Publication is not of much value to either the citizen or lawyer unless it is reliable, and this requires that publications not only reproduce rules exactly as adopted but that they be kept current with respect to modifications of rules. Arrangements for distribution of rules and for the form of reference must be convenient for the user.[7]

Types. Existing rules publication systems are of four general types: (1) those requiring each agency to publish its own rules, either with or without central supervision; (2) those requiring periodic compilation of rules with some central supervision, but without any provision for systematic supplementation between compilations; (3) those requiring periodic compilation of rules and providing for systematic supplementation under central supervision between compilations; and (4) those providing for centrally supervised continual revision based on a loose-leaf compilation with periodic and systematic supplementation of replacement pages.[8]

Types (1) and (2) lack reliability and convenience because they do not provide any systematic or effective means by which interested per-

---

[7] Wisconsin Legislative Council, *1955 Report, Administrative Rule Making*, p. 149.

[8] *Ibid.*, pp. 150-53.

sons may keep abreast of rule changes that occur between compilations. Types (3) and (4) accord more adequately with the requisites of a good system.

Federal system.   The federal system is one of the earliest and best developed of type (3). The rules of federal agencies were compiled in 1938 and recompiled in 1949. The first edition of the *Code of Federal Regulations* contained the rules in effect as of June 1, 1938. It consisted of sixteen bound volumes of rules and an index volume. Since the *Code* was divided into fifty titles, some volumes contained several titles. A cumulative supplement was compiled in 1943, and annual noncumulative supplements, thereafter. The 1949 *Code* is in a more flexible form than its predecessor. Each of its fifty-two bound volumes contains an index and has a pocket for cumulative annual supplements. Rules initially appear in the *Federal Register,* which is issued daily except Sundays, Mondays, and days following holidays. A user of the *Code* can make certain that he has the latest agency rule on a subject by checking three sources: the bound volume of the *Code of Federal Regulations*; the pocket part of that volume; and the *Federal Register.* Each issue of the *Federal Register* is indexed, and a cumulative index is issued approximately every month.[9]

Continual revision.   California and Wisconsin have the only continual-revision rules publication systems in existence. California administrative rules were codified during the period 1945 to 1947. The code was printed in a loose-leaf form for insertion into ring binders. Loose-leaf supplements, comprising pages of the code to be inserted in lieu of pages that contain the superseded or modified rules, are issued every two weeks. If the pages are properly inserted in the code and the corresponding old pages are removed, the user always has a current set of rules at hand and has no need to look at additional volumes or pamphlets.[10] Wisconsin adopted a similar rules publication system in 1955, placing it under the central supervision of the Wisconsin revisor of statutes.[11] It is to be noted that the *Federal*

9 *Ibid.,* pp. 151-52.
10 See 1951 Calif. Gov't. Code and 1953 Supp., sec. 11409 (a).
11 Wis. Stat., sec. 35.93 (1955).

Personnel Manual is also published in a cumulative, loose-leaf, and current-replacement form; but it is not a rules publication.

The continual revision system employed in California and Wisconsin provides a greater degree of flexibility and is more convenient to use than the federal system. The difficulty with the latter is that its register consists simply of a compilation of new rules, and the user must check three sources to be certain that he is current. The loose-leaf system, however, is more expensive.

Scope. A major problem in devising an effective publication system is that of determining its proper scope. It is generally agreed that substantive agency policies—including those which may result in the imposition of a penalty or the loss of, or the failure to gain, a benefit or service—and rules of agency procedure and practice should be published. There are other agency materials, however, with respect to which the question of inclusion or exclusion is more difficult to determine. Among these are various interpretations and statements of general policy formulated by agencies to guide them in their administration of the law, rules of agency organization, forms, instructions, and pertinent statutes.[12] In general, it is considered desirable to achieve as much publicity as possible for these materials, especially if they have general application and affect private rights and interests. The practical question is whether this can be done without unduly hampering administration and without undue expense.

Aside from these general types of agency material, there are specific areas of substantive law where publication of rules and other policy materials as part of an administrative code is of questionable value.

---

[12] A California legislative committee found, for example, numerous instances in which agencies avoided adoption and publication of rules, as defined in the state administrative procedure act, by use of the designations "policies" and "instructions." "The most serious of the evils existing in this type of administrative action," observed the committee, "are the lack of public information as to the action of the department, as they keep such rules or regulations strictly matters of internal procedure, and the lack of public assurance that such interpretations will not be changed overnight" (Senate Interim Committee on Administrative Regulations, *Second Preliminary and Partial Report* [California Senate: Senate Interim Committee, 1953], pp. 13-18, at p. 15).

Such areas include military affairs, international relations, educational institutions, and penal and correctional matters and institutions. The same may be said of rules adequately made known to affected persons by means other than publication in an administrative code or register, such as rules made known by signs or signals in the use of public works, including streets and highways.

The scope of the federal system is largely determined by presidential discretion and the Federal Administrative Procedure Act of 1946. The Federal Register Act uses the generic term "document," defined to include "any Presidential proclamation or Executive order and any order, regulation, rule, certificate, code of fair competition, license, notice, or similar instrument issued, prescribed, or promulgated by a Federal agency. . . ."[13] The act requires publication in the *Federal Register* of (1) all presidential proclamations and executive orders, except those which have no general applicability and legal effect or are effective only against federal agencies, their officers, agents, or employees; (2) documents that the President might determine to have general applicability and legal effect; and (3) documents whose publication may be required by act of Congress. It is stipulated, however, that every document or order that prescribes a penalty must be deemed to have general applicability and legal effect. In addition, publication in the *Federal Register* is required for "such other documents . . . as may be authorized to be published pursuant hereto by regulations prescribed hereunder with the approval of the President. . . ."[14] In the Administrative Procedure Act of 1946, Congress greatly augmented the scope of the federal system by requiring publication of substantive rules in the *Federal Register*.[15]

Supervision. For a rules publication arrangement to have any semblance of being a system, it must have a certain amount of central supervision (the less detail prescribed by statute, the more cen-

---

[13] 44 U. S. C. A. 304 (1953 Supplement).

[14] 44 U. S. C. A. 305 (a) and (b) (1953 Supplement).

[15] "Every agency shall separately state and currently publish in the Federal Register . . . substantive rules as authorized by law . . ." (5 U. S. C. A. 1002 [a] [3]).

tral supervision needed). Among the various functions assigned to supervising bodies or officers are the following: (1) determining the form and numbering of rules submitted for publication; (2) defining the scope of the system; (3) determining the exact times and form of publication; (4) preparing and editing copy for the printer; (5) selling and distributing copies of published rules; (6) prorating costs of publication among agencies; (7) preparing an index for published rules; and (8) providing advice and assistance to agencies with respect to revision and publication of their rules. Some of these functions can be accommodated by careful statutory prescription and, as a matter of fact, no supervising agency or officer presently exercises all of them. Others, such as items (4), (7), and (8), can be properly assumed only by a central supervising agency or officer.

Of course, selection of the officer or agency of a given jurisdiction to supervise a publication system is a matter of situational judgment. In many states, the secretary of state is the choice, since he is usually in charge of the filing of rules. In states that have an office of revisor of statutes or a statutes revision commission, such an agency usually is charged with supervision because of the similarity of techniques required for publication and revision of statutes and rules.

A few states have created special boards for the purpose. This is what the federal government has done. Supervising the federal system is a permanent Administrative Committee of the Federal Register consisting of the Archivist, as chairman; an officer of the Department of Justice designated by the Attorney General; the Public Printer; and the Administrator of General Services, who acts as secretary to the committee. As one of its supervising functions, the committee may, with the President's approval, require publication of "documents" in the *Federal Register* that are not otherwise published under the Federal Register Act.[16]

Central filing. The filing of rules with a central depository is a universal requirement in those jurisdictions which have established a centrally supervised rules publication system. It is also a requirement in some states that have not established any publication system.

[16] 44 U. S. C. A. 302 (1953 Supplement).

While the details of filing vary, most states having a central depository have designated the office of the secretary of state as the depository. The Federal Register Division of the National Archives
Establishment serves as the federal depository.

The original purpose of central filing requirements was probably
that of providing publicity for agency rules. Apparently, this goal has
not been accomplished. In his study of administrative procedure
legislation in a number of states, Professor Ferrel Heady reported
that the rule files were seldom used by members of the public.[17]
However, central filing serves other useful purposes. Requiring agencies to file all their rules with a central depository is almost indis-
pensable to the successful operation of a centrally supervised rules
publication system. Moreover, central filing is a means of giving official status to a rule and of providing certain presumptions of its legality and authenticity. States that have a central filing requirement
provide that a rule is not effective until it has been filed. The Federal
Register Act has a similar provision.

It is well established that the presumption of validity which courts
regularly accord legislative enactments attaches also to administrative
rules. For example, Mr. Justice Brandeis stated this doctrine for the
United States Supreme Court in 1935:

> . . . where the regulation is within the scope of authority legally dele-
> gated, the presumption of the existence of facts justifying its specific
> exercise attaches alike to statutes, to municipal ordinances, and to
> orders of administrative bodies.[18]

Accordingly, when a responsible agency official files a rule with a
central depository, and it is accompanied by a certificate attesting
that the file copy is a duplicate of the original adopted by the agency,
the presumption normally attaches that the rule is authentic and
that it was duly adopted pursuant to prescribed procedures. The

17 Heady, *Administrative Procedure Legislation in the States*, p. 29.
18 Pacific States Box & Basket Co. v. White, 296 U. S. 176, 186 (1935). For confirmation that such a presumption likewise may attach to acts of municipal administrative and legislative bodies, see Ernest R. Bartley and William W. Boyer,
Municipal Zoning: Florida Law and Practice (Gainesville, Fla.: Public Administration Clearing Service, University of Florida, 1950), pp. 49-64.

agency benefits from central filing in the added protection afforded its rule against possible attacks on its legality. The public also benefits, for the presumption attaching to an agency's rules by virtue of their being centrally filed serves as an inducement for an agency to file and publish its policies as rules.

Delayed effective date. Closely related to the filing and publication of rules is the problem of when to make them effective. The objective of the delayed effective date requirement is to make a rule, in its final form, available and known to interested persons prior to its taking effect. Several states have attempted to achieve this objective by providing that rules do not become effective until the elapse of a period of time, ranging from ten to thirty days, after they have been filed or published.[19] Exceptions are made for emergency situations. Such provisions do not operate successfully, however, unless they are integrated with the publication of a periodic register.[20] Ideally, the system should be so devised that the register will be in the hands of interested persons before the rules contained therein are made effective.

In order for the devices of publication, filing, and the delayed effective date to be most successful in providing publicity for administrative policies, each device should be an integral part of one carefully planned rules publication system.

STIMULATING PUBLICATION

It is not unusual for an agency subject to a central rules publication system to neglect or to decide not to publish as rules at least some of its policies, even if such policies accord with the legislature's

[19] Illinois, Missouri, and Ohio provide that rules do not become effective until ten days after filing. See Ill. Stat., ch. 127, sec. 266 (1953, State Bar Ass'n. Ed.); Mo. Stat. Ann., sec. 536.020 (2) (Vernon, 1953); Ohio Code, sec. 119.04 (1953). California, Minnesota, and South Dakota provide for a thirty-day delay. See 1951 Calif. Gov't. Code and 1953 Supp., sec. 11422; Minn. Stat., sec. 15.042 (4) (1953); S. Dak. Code, sec. 65.0106 (1939).

[20] Thus, Wisconsin makes a rule effective on the first day of the month following its publication in the Wisconsin administrative register unless a statute stipulates otherwise, a later date is prescribed by the agency, the rule is an emergency rule, or by some contingency publication of an issue of the register is delayed. See Wis. Stat., sec. 227.026 (1) and (3) (1955).

definition of a "rule" and are not among those exempt from rules publication requirements. Indeed, it is quite possible that a skilled investigator could uncover many examples of such unpublished policies in *any* agency bound by rules publication requirements. This was found to be the case in Wisconsin, which is known for its progressive state government.[21]

Perhaps the basic reason for nonpublication is not willful dereliction on the part of administrators, but rather the disparities between law and practice that almost always exist within the administrative process. It is easy for administrators to tend to ignore their responsibilities with respect to general administrative procedure requirements when they have trouble enough in fulfilling their specific day-to-day responsibilities involving major agency purposes. It is not easy, however, for many administrators to engage in the kind of introspection necessary to discover and crystallize all generally applicable policies obscured by daily tasks and events.

Most agencies develop policy approaches to particular types of problems that recur more or less frequently. Seldom are such general policies published as rules, and occasionally they are not even reduced to writing. Yet they may, and often do, determine whether, for example, a person will obtain a license or similar privilege or benefit. Frequently, they appear in the form of manuals or separate staff instructions, which are sometimes labeled as "not intended for public use" or "for use of agency personnel only."[22] The federal Attorney General's Committee on Administrative Procedure was quite critical of the refusal of agencies to publicize policies incorporated in such manuals:

> Rarely, if at all, is there justification for such a practice.... The Committee is strongly of the opinion that, with possible rare exceptions, whenever a policy has crystallized with an agency sufficiently to be embodied in a memorandum or instruction to the staff, the interests of

[21] Wisconsin Legislative Council, *1955 Report, Administrative Rule Making*, pp. 65-68.

[22] *Ibid.* See also California's experience in this respect in *op. cit. supra*, note 12 of this chapter.

fairness, clarity, and efficiency suggest that it be put into the form of a definite opinion or instruction and published as such. . . .[23]

If an agency fails to publish its well-established policies and interpretations as rules, notwithstanding requirements that it do so, the affected public is denied its right to know what agency law is. Consequently, the basic question here is: Can an agency be encouraged or compelled to promulgate such policies? Can it be required to ferret out its hidden law?

Coercion by the legislature? It would be possible, of course, to define the term "rule" to include generally applicable policies and interpretations, as many procedure acts do, and then to provide that rules are not valid until filed and published. Generally applicable policies and interpretations that had not been filed and published would then presumably be invalid. Such a solution, however, is not as simple and effective as it appears at first glance.

One difficulty is that an agency could proceed indefinitely to give effect to its unfiled and unpublished policies without their being contested, and their legality determined, in court. Another is that not all policies or interpretations should be included in a definition of "rule." No student of administration would dissent from the view that it is proper for every agency to develop some policy on a case-by-case basis. When there has been no administrative experience in a particular field on which to rely, development of the detailed aspects of general agency policy invariably proceeds in this manner. Furthermore, the legislature's policy in a new field is often couched in such general terms as "immoral or unprofessional conduct," "in the course of employment," "public convenience and necessity," or "in the public interest." Detailed agency policies amplifying the meaning of such inexplicit standards can hardly be formulated on the basis of two or three cases. Only well-established agency policies and interpretations should be treated, filed, and published as rules.

An additional difficulty immediately arises. When has an agency policy or interpretation become so well established that it should be

[23] Committee on Administrative Procedure, *Final Report of the Attorney General's Committee on Administrative Procedure*, p. 29.

treated as a rule? One possible answer is: when the policy has been reduced to writing and is being followed by the agency in the administration of the law. We have observed that such policies often appear in the form of staff instructions, guides, or agency manuals for field personnel. Others appear in written form in the minutes of the agency's policy board, if any, and in agency correspondence with members of the public and legislators. Policies of federal field establishments can also be found in reports to agency headquarters, Congress, the Civil Service Commission, and other outside bodies; agency directives that are not dignified by being bound in volumes and indexed; inspection reports by the General Accounting Office, the Civil Service Commission, and headquarters analysts; congressional committee hearings and reports, which are usually published verbatim; study and survey reports by outside management consultants, and other management literature; budget statements; and internal audit reports. Though all these policies are reduced to written or printed form and are followed by agencies, and many of them affect the private rights and interests of general classes of citizens, they are seldom published as agency rules.

The view that a policy should be treated as a rule when it has been reduced to writing fails to recognize that many important agency policies are never reduced to writing. Moreover, such policies are frequently followed more rigidly than those which have been put into written form.

Unwritten policies are more prevalent in agencies with a single head than in those with a board or commission form of organization. The single administrator is the final policy-making authority as well as the chief administrator, and, particularly with respect to his own policy decisions, he is less likely to feel a compulsion to reduce agency policies to written form and to make them public. Policies in the board or commission form of agency organization are more likely to be reduced to written form, if only for the reason that they may be shared among the board members or commissioners. It is to be noted, however, that agency boards or commissions are often created to perform quasi-judicial functions rather than to make generally

applicable policies, and in such instances they usually prefer to proceed on a case-by-case adjudicatory basis rather than by rule making.

In any event, perhaps all general policies that have been adopted
by an agency for its future guidance in deciding specific cases should
be treated as rules and made known to those affected by them. But
it is very doubtful whether a legislature can effectively compel an
agency to disinter these policies and publish them. In the final analysis, it is up to the agency to declare what its policies are.

Absence of judicial sanctions.   Assume that a legislature has been
able to draw distinctions between policies which should be filed and
published as rules and those which should not, and that it has directed the courts to invalidate an unfiled and unpublished policy of
the former category. There would still exist the problem of how such
legislation can be effectively enforced. An adequate remedy would
be provided in cases concerning policies that seek to impose a fine
or forfeiture or to require the doing of some act. If the agency policy
is declared invalid because it has not been filed and published as a
rule, as required by law, the court will not order the payment of the
fine or the doing of the act.[24] The complainant has an adequate judicial remedy, therefore, and the agency is subjected to a powerful inducement to file and publish such policies as rules.

Suppose, however, that the unpublished policies operate to deny
a benefit rather than to impose a duty. Many administrative policies
operate to grant or deny some type of administrative consent or permission. Benefits may be denied through the refusal to issue licenses
and permits or to grant loans, subsidies, or aids of various kinds. In
such cases a judicial declaration to the effect that the agency policy
is invalid does not help the complainant. An order of the court directing the agency to grant the license or other benefit would be needed
to redress a complainant's grievance. But courts seldom issue such

---

[24] See, for example, Hotch v. United States, 212 F. 2d 280 (C. A. 9, 1954), in which
the court held invalid a Department of Interior regulation prohibiting fishing in
certain "closed" waters because it was not published as required. The court ruled
that the rules publication requirements of the Administrative Procedure Act and
the Federal Register Act must be read as a part of every congressional delegation of
authority unless specifically excepted.

orders, because of the general judicial doctrine that mandamus will not lie to compel an officer to perform an act when the officer has been given discretion by statute regarding performance of the act. And, of course, injunction is even further removed as an appropriate remedy.[25] Thus, judicial invalidation of an unpublished policy statement that operates to deny a benefit does not result in a requirement that the agency grant the benefit. In short, there appears to be no judicial remedy within the American system of jurisprudence compelling a government agency to file and publish such policy statements. Here, then, is a loophole in the fabric of justice that permits administrative wrongs for which no legal remedy exists.

External audit.   The absence or inadequacy of judicial sanctions makes it necessary to consider other possible means of inducing agencies to adopt their generally applicable policies as rules. One such means would be to establish a central body, such as a department of administrative procedure, and to authorize it to audit externally the substance and procedures of agency action with the purpose of ferreting out hidden agency law—policies that the agency should promulgate as rules. On the basis of such audits, the department of administrative procedure could recommend corrective action to the agencies. The department could be so structured as to be made responsible to the legislature.[26] The legislature would then be provided with opportunities to reexamine basic agency policy in the light of administrative experience, and to determine whether administrative discretion should be restricted by greater statutory detail or permitted to continue relatively unfettered.

To be effective, external auditing of administrative policy making would have to be continuous. The substantive law of administrative agencies is changeable, complex, and technical. Reexamination would be a difficult and time-consuming process. But even with such a con-

---

[25] One noted authority is so critical of all extraordinary common law remedies, in terms of their adequacy for review of administrative action, that he proposes abolishing them by establishing instead "a single, simple form of proceeding for all review of administrative action" (Davis, *Administrative Law and Government* [1960], p. 380).

[26] See the discussion of a proposal for such a department in Chapter 7.

tinuous central audit, the fact remains that the exercise of administrative discretion cannot be made responsible by statutory restrictions of express policy-making powers so long as administrative agencies have extensive discretionary authority to decide individual cases. Such discretion appears necessary for the effective functioning of government. Moreover, it is difficult to conceive how a department of administrative procedure or a legislature can compel an agency to substitute rule making for a case-by-case approach without perverting agency purposes and goals, especially when the agency is engaged in the granting or withholding of consent or benefits.

Legislative scrutiny. Another possibility is for the legislature to establish a committee to investigate the administrative process for unpublished policies. But this would seem to be a haphazard endeavor, because the same difficulties confronting a department of administrative procedure would be accentuated for a legislative committee.[27]

In all too many instances, it is possible for an agency to ignore hearing and publication requirements, and other provisions of an administrative procedure act, by the simple expedient of formulating its policies as unpublished policy statements rather than published rules. When considering control devices, therefore, it is important that the legislature seek means to encourage the publication of those unpublished policy statements that an agency enforces as law. Provisions relating to the definition of "rule," the hearing requirement, and the rules publication system can be framed to *stimulate* such publication. But it is doubtful, under the best conditions, that a legislature can effectively and reasonably *compel* publication of unpublished policies operating to grant, withhold, or deny licenses, permits, benefits, or any type of administrative consent.

The necessity for administrative discretion may run counter to, and frustrate, any legislative or other attempt to assure publication of all unpublished agency policy statements given legal force. The task of ferreting out hidden law and making it known to affected

27 The subject of legislative scrutiny is discussed more extensively in Chapter 6.

persons is not an easy one. It is probable that the public's right to know can never be fully secured in this respect. This is a problem for which no sure solution exists. Yet it merits considerable study, for it is crucial to democracy in public administration.

Chapter Five

Adjudication
and
Other Problems

POLICY MAKING BY ADJUDICATION

As has been suggested, agency policy can be formed by a case-by-case approach. When an agency has discretion to proceed both by rule making and by adjudication, there is usually no reason why it cannot choose to proceed by adjudication and virtually ignore its rule-making authority.

An agency that functions by adjudication evolves unstated general policies that are often discoverable only by exhaustive research into its maze of decided cases. The discovery of such policies is a challenge to both the lay citizen and the agency itself. It represents such a formidable challenge to the legal profession as to require many of its members to devote their entire careers to mastering the mysteries of particular fields of adjudication, to the exclusion of all other professional interests.

There is no question that administrative agencies should adopt and publish as rules the general policies developed by them in the course of deciding individual cases. Only then will persons who expect to have dealings with an agency be informed of the objectives of its regulation. Only then will the agency equip itself with adequate guides and frames of reference by which it may effectively project and program its own administrative needs, establish its goals, and develop a logical and reasonably consistent regulatory scheme. For the citizen, the problem is essentially his right to know. For public administration, it is essentially a problem of administrative efficiency and public responsibility.

Enough has been said concerning the public's right to know of what agency law consists. But what of the problem of administrative efficiency and the general public interest related to it?

Federal regulatory commissions. As problems of national security and economic growth become ever more critical and multi-dimensional, and as the impact of technology on social problems becomes more complex, the need to clarify the objectives of government regulation becomes more urgent. Without such clarification, regulatory activity will continue to flounder in aimlessness.

Federal regulatory commissions are afflicted with the disease of aimlessness to a greater extent than other administrative establishments. The Civil Aeronautics Board, for example, has direction and control of one great segment of the national transportation system. Yet its functioning lacks any coordination with the Interstate Commerce Commission, which regulates the railroads, truck lines, and barge lines; nor is either clearly responsible to the President or Congress. The very independence of the independent regulatory commissions prevents formulation of an effective national transportation policy. The problems of urban transportation alone, in all their dimensions, may be beyond the competence of individual administrative agencies in terms of adequate solutions. But certainly if these agencies continue to proceed by adjudication without codification, then agency policy bases and administrative experience, upon which overall government programs can be grounded and framed, will be lacking.

Building policy bridges. Though the federal Attorney General's Committee on Administrative Procedure concluded in 1941 that rule making should be encouraged so as to reduce the need for case-by-case adjudications,[1] the powerful American Bar Association has accelerated its efforts to judicialize further the administrative process.[2] No one disputes the advantages of the case-by-case approach in meeting particular exigencies, but it has the great disadvantage of obscuring the principles of regulation by which administrative agencies themselves should be governed. To distill these principles from the welter of decided cases is a very difficult task. Too often, legislatures set forth the standards to guide administrative agencies only in the most general terms. Bridges must be built between these general statutory standards and the particular cases that agencies are called upon to decide. Only by formulating administrative rules will agencies erect these bridges.

Moreover, by crystallizing and publishing the various policies threaded through the labyrinth of case decisions, administrative agencies would serve a number of other desirable purposes. There could be more intelligent discussion by the legislature, the agencies, the affected interests, and the general public of the objectives of regulation and the means to achieve them. Disclosure of the needs of, and preparation for changes in, administrative programs would be facilitated. Particular cases could be decided more quickly, and the training of new personnel in administrative tasks and responsibilities could be improved.

Private interests would also benefit if agency policies and objectives were clearly defined for them. They would be enabled to cooperate more fully with the agencies in the achievement of announced policy goals, in the formulation of which they would presumably have had an opportunity to participate.

Such clarification has other advantages, as well as disadvantages, as one scholar has observed:

[1] Committee on Administrative Procedure, *Final Report of the Attorney General's Committee on Administrative Procedure*, p. 258. See also discussion of the "Hector Memorandum" and the CAB and notes 14 and 15 in Chapter 6.

[2] Ferrel Heady, "The New Reform Movement in Regulatory Administration," *Public Administration Review*, XIX (Spring 1959), 89-100, 93.

While consistency is not an end in itself, it is important for all concerned to know whether apparent inconsistency is due to a change in policy or discriminatory action. Finally, there is no reason why the elaboration of administrative standards need stand in the way of desirable changes in policy. On the contrary, it will facilitate change by making it easier to identify undesirable or unworkable policies. All this is not to minimize the difficulties that will be faced in the attempt to work out more specific regulatory standards. . . .[3]

THE ETHICS OF INFLUENCE

Since 1887, when Congress created the Interstate Commerce Commission, many federal regulatory bodies have been created. Among these are a number of independent regulatory commissions established to regulate various segments of the nation's economic life. Though commission members are presidential appointees, they enjoy considerable independence from the executive branch because their terms of office exceed that of the President and he may not remove them except for cause as stated by statute.[4] In 1957, the House of Representatives established the Subcommittee on Legislative Oversight to make the first broad inquiry into whether these agencies were carrying out congressional intent. One of the ways in which this committee has had an impact is illustrated by the following news summary of March 13, 1960:

In its relatively short life, the committee has taken three prominent Government scalps. The first two were those of Richard A. Mack of the Federal Communications Commission, who resigned two years ago and is now under Federal indictment on charges of conspiring to influence the award of a television channel; and Sherman Adams, The Assistant to the President, who resigned under political fire for accepting favors and gifts from Bernard Goldfine, whose affairs were under scrutiny by Federal regulatory agencies. The third scalp was that of John C. Doer-

[3] Carl A. Auerbach, "The Regulation of Motor Carriers in Wisconsin," *Wisconsin Law Review* (March 1951), 231-243, at p. 343.
[4] Humphrey's Executor (Rathbun) v. United States, 295 U. S. 602 (1935).

fer, chairman of the F. C. C. since 1957. Last week Mr. Doerfer quit under fire by the subcommittee.[5]

The Doerfer affair.　The circumstances leading to Chairman Doerfer's resignation are symptomatic of a problem that has major implications for administrative policy making. When the House subcommittee first began looking into FCC practices in 1958, it charged that FCC members, including Mr. Doerfer, engaged in "constant fraternization" with officials of the broadcasting industry. Questions were raised concerning how the FCC exercised its authority to regulate the communications industry through its power to license broadcasters. Mr. Doerfer testified at length at various hearings held by the subcommittee. Early in 1960, it was learned that Mr. Doerfer had spent a week's vacation aboard the yacht of the owner of a dozen radio and television stations and had accepted other expensive favors.

Mr. Doerfer defended his behavior by saying that a commissioner need not be a "second-class citizen" and be "cloistered" from social activities of his own choosing. There was no intimation that the owner of the yacht, his host, was a party of interest in any contested proceeding before the FCC. Nevertheless, subcommittee Democrats criticized his attitude, and Republicans and administration aides became increasingly disturbed by the prospect of an election-year "corruption in government" issue. After being summoned to the White House, Mr. Doerfer wrote to the President that he would not waver from his view that his actions were correct, but that he was resigning "to avoid possible embarrassment to you and your Administration." The President replied that he thought Mr. Doerfer's decision "wise."[6]

If there were no more than this to the Doerfer affair, the incident would appear closed. However, the problem, of which Doerfer's resignation is symptomatic, is much deeper, more subtle, and more complex.

Off-the-record contacts.　In June 1959, hearings before the Subcommittee on Legislative Oversight were addressed in part to this basic question:

[5] *New York Times,* March 13, 1960, sec. 4, p. 2.
[6] *Ibid.*

What legislative or administrative measures have been or should be taken to preclude attempts to influence Commission members or employees by means which do not afford a fair opportunity to interested persons materially affected by Commission action to present their case, and at the same time preserve the necessary access by the Commission to information from the public, the regulated industry and others?[7]

FCC Chairman Doerfer attempted to answer this question. The following exchange between him and Congressman William L. Springer is quite revealing:

MR. DOERFER. . . . The essence of this question is whether ex parte representations or extraordinary information common to adjudicatory proceedings should be extended to rulemaking proceedings of administrative agencies. My position is that it should not be extended to rulemaking proceedings. To do so would be to change the very purpose for which administrative agencies were established. . . . If all matters are to be made a matter of record and no information obtained or obtainable by Commissioners or their employees outside of a record, there would be little left of the administrative process as we understand it. . . .

I submit that really what is at issue and what this committee should consider . . . is whether, in fact, some adjudicatory matters may be disposed of by the Commission under the guise of rule making. I have no quarrel with that at all.

MR. SPRINGER. Mr. Doerfer, do I understand that we are all agreed that there should be no contact, conversation, either by telephone or letter, upon contested matters? Is that right? . . .

MR. DOERFER. I am in agreement with that.

MR. SPRINGER. . . . Are you in effect saying that all of those matters that are not contested are, in effect, ex parte proceedings . . . , including rule making, which you may talk with people in the industry about, the public, or an attorney who may have information about the subject, or anybody else? . . .

MR. DOERFER. Well, Congressman, I think you put your finger on what is the real problem today, and that is the definition of what should be or is adjudication.

[7] *Major Administrative Process Problems*, Hearings before a Subcommittee of the Committee on Interstate and Foreign Commerce, House of Representatives, 86th Cong., 1st sess., Panel Discussion by Representatives of the Government, and of the Bar, June 16, 1959.

MR. SPRINGER. That is what I am trying to get, the division, where the dividing line is. I did not get it clearly from your statement.

MR. DOERFER. Maybe I can answer it this way: Rulemaking, in my concept, is nothing more or less than policymaking. It is an indication to the industry, the bar, the public and the Congress, what this Commission proposes to do in the future, given a certain set of facts or a certain situation. In that field is where the Commission should be absolutely without any restraint, to get all the information it possibly can.[8]

At least five propositions may be extracted from Mr. Doerfer's testimony: (1) Judicialization of the administrative process with respect to adjudications should not be projected to rule making. (2) When an agency is engaged in rule making (which is essentially policy making), it should not be restrained in its off-the-record contacts with the public. (3) On the other hand, there should be no off-the-record contacts between the agency and the public on the merits of matters being contested in agency adjudications. (4) Case-by-case adjudications could be reduced to make way for more rule making. (5) But there is no general agreement as to the proper dividing line between rule making and adjudication. These propositions deserve examination.

Mr. Doerfer's contention that rule making should not be judicialized is supported by our discussion of the nature of agency policy making. Though agency policy making is organized and purposeful in its comprehensive dimensions, and hence capable of descriptive analysis, it must be flexible and situational. Administrators cannot, and should not, "wear the blinders of judges" when "legislating."[9] Not only should they be free to enter into contact with the public when formulating policies, as Mr. Doerfer contended, but environ-

[8] *Ibid.*, pp. 104-8.

[9] With respect to the federal regulatory commissions, one Washington journalist has commented: "The first need is to recognize that the large issues before the agencies in their rule-making role are political in nature. They require political solutions—the adjustment of a variety of economic and social interests—something very different from the decision of a court case confined in a legal record.

"At the least, then, it is clear that to be effective as legislators the agencies cannot wear the blinders of judges" (Anthony Lewis, "To Regulate the Regulators," *New York Times Magazine*, February 22, 1959, pp. 66-67).

mental interaction, which is essential to agency policy making, is best reflected by policy initiation and public participation, most of which occurs in an informal rather than a formal manner. Indeed, the extent to which public administration accommodates participation in its policy making may determine how "public" it is.[10]

However, Mr. Doerfer seemed to be saying that to prohibit off-the-record contacts in rule making would destroy the administrative process. It is certainly not judicialization of the rule-making process to require that some sort of record be maintained of all contacts with the public that are germane to agency policy formulation. Whether administrators have these contacts through informal conferences or consultations, including fortuitous meetings, or through advisory committees and public hearings, they should record the nature of the contacts, including information concerning the participants and the essence of what is discussed. Moreover, any written materials submitted to them, including correspondence, can easily be made a matter of record. Efficient administrators normally keep such records in any event, whether by filing or other means. By doing so, they are not made less free in contacting members of the public. Indeed, in terms of responsible and effective public administration, there is justification for extending such a requirement to include intragovernmental and intergovernmental, as well as public, contacts.

A general legislative requirement to this effect, regardless of its enforceability, would at least have the salutary influence of stimulating administrators to be more conscious of the desirability of recording all external contacts.[11] On the other hand, there appears to be no justification for requiring, in a general administrative procedure act, that all agencies maintain an evidentiary type of record, common to adjudicatory proceedings, in their rule making. If a legislature concludes that particular kinds of rule making are litigious enough in character to warrant the governance of adjudicatory or court-like

[10] See Chapter 8.

[11] See *Administrative Practice and Procedure*, Report of U. S. Senate Committee on the Judiciary made by its Subcommittee on Administrative Practice and Procedure, pursuant to S. Res. 61, 86th Cong., 2nd sess., Report no. 1484 (Washington, D. C.: U. S. Gov't. Printing Office, May 25, 1960).

procedures, it can impose such procedures in individual statutes tailored to fit the agencies concerned rather than by general procedural legislation.[12]

Few would disagree with the proposition that all external contacts on the merits of matters contested in adjudicatory proceedings should be made part of a formal record. Otherwise, when administrators are acting as judges, the ideal of the independence of the judiciary—so fundamental in Western jurisprudence—may be perverted. It should be noted that Mr. Doerfer's "forced" resignation was considered justified not because his benefactor was a party of interest in a contested case before the FCC, for he was not, but because Mr. Doerfer was thought to have accepted expensive favors from a member of his agency's affected clientele. It is widely believed that, as a necessary price one must pay for holding public trust, a public officer should not accept any expensive personal favor or gift from any member of the public.

Congress and other legislative bodies have not enacted legislation of the sort recommended by the 1951 Senate subcommittee chaired by Senator Paul H. Douglas to improve ethical standards in the federal government.[13] Unethical administrative behavior in its various

12 See, for example, proposed legislation and discussions thereon in *Independent Regulatory Agencies Legislation*, Hearings before the Committee on Interstate and Foreign Commerce, House of Representatives, 86th Cong., 2d sess. (Washington, D. C.: U. S. Gov't. Printing Office, March 15, 16, 18, 22, 23, 25, 29, 30, 31, April 1, 4, 7, and 8, 1960).

13 *Ethical Standards in Government*, Report of the U. S. Senate Subcommittee of the Committee on Labor and Public Welfare, Proposals for Improvement of Ethical Standards in the Federal Government including Establishment of a Commission on Ethics in Government, 82d Cong., 1st sess. See Paul H. Douglas, "Improvement of Ethical Standards in the Federal Government: Problems and Proposals," *Annals of the American Academy of Political and Social Science*, CCLXXX (March 1952), 149-57; and the statement of Senator Douglas in which he argues for prohibition of ex parte communications in rule making as well as in adjudicatory proceedings, in *Administrative Procedure Legislation*, Hearings before the U. S. Senate Subcommittee on Administrative Practice and Procedure of the Committee on the Judiciary, 86th Cong., 1st sess., pursuant to S. Res. 61 (Washington, D. C.: U. S. Gov't. Printing Office, July 21, 22, 23, 1959 and Nov. 19, 20, 1959), pp. 25-33. See also discussion of "ex parte approaches" in James M. Landis, *Report on Regulatory Agencies to the President-Elect* (Washington, D. C.: U. S. Gov't. Printing Office, December 1960), pp. 13-15. During April 1961, President Kennedy, in response to the Landis report, sent two special messages to Congress calling for cer-

forms has not been clearly defined and proscribed by law, whether it attends rule making, adjudication, or other administrative activity. The advantages of relying more on rule making and less on adjudication, as suggested by Mr. Doerfer, have already been discussed. Rule making permits the building of policy bridges between decided cases and broad, legislatively prescribed standards. It permits clarification of the objectives of regulation and the development of logical schemes of regulation. Mr. Doerfer's suggestion was well taken, for the need to reap these advantages is nowhere more apparent than in the field of communications regulation. Moreover, unethical influences attach less to rule making than to adjudication, because rule making commends a large measure of freedom in making external contacts, whereas any contacts off the record in adjudicatory proceedings are tantamount to favoritism or inequitable treatment of the parties of interest. The circumstances surrounding Mr. Doerfer's resignation do not obscure the fact that his suggestion was made at a time when "payola," "rigged TV quizzes," and "influence peddling" were becoming household terms throughout the nation.

A Problem of Definition

Many authorities agree that freedom to make public contacts generally should be permitted or encouraged in rule making but judicially circumscribed in adjudication, while favoritism should be forbidden throughout public administration. Few additional problems would exist were there general agreement as to the proper dividing line between rule making and adjudication. To define rule making simply as policy making that indicates what an agency proposes to do in the future, as Mr. Doerfer did, fails to provide an adequate distinction.

---

tain reforms in the federal regulatory commissions. The first message was directed to greater coordination among the agencies and the necessity for "formulation of the rationale underlying important agency decisions," among other proposed remedies. The second message called for revision and strengthening of federal conflict of interest laws, including dealing with the problem of ex parte communication, which the President labeled "one of the most complex in the entire field of Government regulation." See the *New York Times*, April 14, 1961, p. 12, and April 28, 1961, p. 16.

The "gray" area. Some agencies proceed exclusively by adjudication and yet manage to indicate in the course of their decisions what they propose to do in the future. And their decisions, though directed, like court decisions, to specific parties rather than to general classes, have far-reaching and general legal force not unlike that of statutes. The National Labor Relations Board, for example, in effect substantively amended the Taft-Hartley Act by this process, as witness the following excerpt from one of its case decisions:

> We have determined that in future cases the Board will assert jurisdiction over transportation operations or other local activities which constitute a link in the chain of interstate commerce only where the annual income received by the particular company involved from services which constitute a part of interstate commerce totals no less than $100,000.[14]

Though addressed to specific parties, the effect of this decision was to deny the right of collective bargaining and other Taft-Hartley protections against unfair labor and management practices to both employees and employers of all trucking firms throughout the nation and the territories whose interstate business does not exceed $100,000 in value per year. By resort to adjudication, the NLRB similarly withheld its jurisdiction from other interstate segments of the economy if they fell below stated dollar standards. Various categories of business have been affected, including retail establishments, utilities, newspapers, the communications industry, and office buildings.[15]

All federal regulatory commissions, and many state regulatory bodies, make decisions by adjudication that indirectly affect general

[14] Breeding Transfer Company, 110 NLRB No. 64.

[15] See John P. Henderson, "The 'No Man's Land' Between State and Federal Jurisdiction," *Labor Law Journal* (September 1957), pp. 587-98, and "The Impact of the NLRB upon Union Growth," *Labor Law Journal* (May 1956), pp. 276-85. For a detailed summary of the board's jurisdiction in terms of various dollar standards, see *Twenty-First Annual Report of the National Labor Relations Board for the Fiscal Year Ended June 30, 1956* (Washington, D. C.: U. S. Gov't. Printing Office, 1957), pp. 7-28. For critical analysis of the board's failure to utilize its rule-making powers, see Cornelius J. Peck, "The Atrophied Rule-Making Powers of the National Labor Relations Board," *Yale Law Journal*, LXX (April 1961), 729-61.

classes of persons and interests. When the Civil Aeronautics Board gives or withholds its consent for an airline to serve a particular community, its decision affects all potential users of such service. When agencies are engaged in rate fixing, price fixing, and the making of similar determinations, the broad and general effect of their decisions may be even more apparent. When the Pennsylvania Public Utilities Commission approves an application of the Equitable Gas Company for an increased rate, all consumers serviced by the company must pay the increased rate.

Congressional committees and their expert witnesses have labored long and hard over the problem of this so-called "gray" area, and apparently without arriving at any iron-clad, mutually exclusive definitions capable of distinguishing rule making from adjudication. It may be argued that it is impossible to devise such definitions, and that ultimately each agency must have discretion to decide and make known at the initiation of a proceeding whether it is to be a rule-making or an adjudicatory proceeding. If the proceeding is to be adjudicatory, then the agency would submit to the judicial restraints required by the legislature and the courts for the duration of the proceeding.

To maintain, however, that an agency should have complete discretion to determine whether each of its proceedings shall be rule-making or adjudicatory is to deny that a legislature can contribute any guidance on such questions. The fact is that it is possible to arrive at reasonable definitions that reduce the "gray" area to the point at which unethical and irresponsible administrative behavior is circumscribed in the interests of integrity of the administrative process and fairness to the public.

Definitions. The definitions of "rule" found in the administrative procedure acts of the state and federal governments can be divided into two or three general types. Most definitions are similar in that they define "rule" in positive terms as, for example, a rule as a statement of agency policy "of general applicability," or "to govern its organization" or "to implement" or "make specific" the law enforced or administered by it.[16] The Kansas, Kentucky, and Michigan acts, on the other hand, define "rule" in such negative terms as, for example: "rule means any rule, regulation or standard except. . . ."[17] A few definitions cannot be classified as belonging to either category.[18] In other words, no common definition of "rule" exists.

An attempt, in the abstract, to arrive at a precise definition of a rule seems futile, but the merits of certain common provisions of the definitions found in the various procedure acts can be discussed with profit. The point upon which most procedure acts agree is that rules relating solely to the management of the internal affairs of the agency are excluded from the definition of a rule. From the standpoint of public hearing and publication requirements, there can be little quarrel with such an exception. Another common provision is that the rule must be of "general application." This phrase is descriptive, in a general way, of rules that are made subject to an administrative procedure act, but it is not precise enough to reduce the "gray" area. The Kansas provision is more specific. It provides that a rule is exempt if it is "directed to a specifically named person or to a group of persons, and does not apply generally throughout the state" or is "duly served by the state agency in the manner authorized by the law upon the person or persons designated therein as the party or parties legally affected."[19] A few jurisdictions qualify the definition of a rule by providing that a rule must be of "future effect."[20] Like the term "general applicability," this phrase is descriptive in a general way but is not of much help in reducing the twilight zone. We have ob-

---

[16] Ariz. Laws, Chap. 97, sec. 3 (1952); Calif. Gov't. Code, sec. 11371 (b) (1951); Ill. Stat., Chap. 127, sec. 264 (1953, State Bar Ass'n. Ed.); Iowa Code Ann., sec. 17A,1 (1953 Supp.); Minn. Stat., sec. 15.041 (4) (1953); Mo. Stat. Ann., sec. 536.010 (2) (Vernon, 1953); Neb. Stat., sec. 84-901 (2) (1943; Reissue of 1950); N. Dak. Code, sec. 28-3201 (2) (1943); Pa. Stat. Ann., Tit. 71, sec. 1710.2 (e) (1953 Supplement); Va. Code Ann., sec. 9-6.2 (b) (1953 Supplement); 60 U. S. Stat. 237, sec. 2 (c) (1946).

[17] Kans. Stat., sec. 77-405 (3) (Corrick, 1949); Ky. Stat., sec. 13.080 (2) (1953); Mich. Stat. Ann., sec. 3.560 (7) (1952).

[18] Ohio Code, sec. 119.01 (C) (1953); Ore. Comp. Laws, sec. 89-501 (1943 Supplement).

[19] Kans. Stat., sec. 77-405 (3) (c) and (d) (Corrick, 1949).

[20] Ariz. Laws, Chap. 97, sec. 3 (1952); Mo. Stat. Ann., sec. 536.010 (2) (Vernon, 1953); 60 U. S. Stat. 237, sec. 2 (c) (1946).

served that orders deciding specific cases, such as those of the NLRB, which presumably are excluded from a definition of a rule, may also have general applicability and be of future effect.

What makes the federal definition so confusing to congressional committees and others is that it includes too much. Not only is a federal rule an agency statement of "general applicability," but it is also one of "particular applicability and future effect designed to implement, interpret, or prescribe law or policy." Moreover, it includes the approval or prescription for the future "of rates, wages, corporate or financial structures or reorganizations thereof, prices, facilities, appliances, services or allowances therefor or of valuations, costs, or accounting, or practices bearing upon any of the foregoing."[21] Then the federal legislation defines an "order" to be simply the final disposition "in any matter other than rule making but including licensing," and "adjudication" to mean "agency process for the formulation of an order."[22] What the federal act does is to make many rule-making proceedings adversary in character. If the fixing of wages, rates, prices, and the other specific references in its definition of a rule were to be redefined as adjudicatory, then the federal "gray" area would be greatly reduced.

In effect, this is what the Wisconsin act does. It defines a rule and then states certain exceptions, among which are those pertaining to adjudication:

227.01 DEFINITIONS. In this chapter:

2. "Contested case" means a proceeding before an agency which, after hearing required by law, the legal rights, duties or privileges of any party to such proceeding are determined or directly affected by a decision or order in such proceeding and in which the assertion by one party of any such right, duty or privilege is denied or controverted by another party to such proceeding.

3. "Rule" means a regulation, standard, statement of policy or general order (including the amendment or repeal of any of the foregoing), of general application and having the effect of law, issued by an agency to implement, interpret or make specific legislation enforced or ad-

21 60 U. S. Stat. 237, sec. 2 (c) (1946).
22 60 U. S. Stat. 237, sec. 2 (d).

ministered by such agency or to govern the organization or procedure
of such agency. . . .

4. . . . *The fact that a statement of policy or an interpretation of a
statute is made in the decision of a case or in an agency decision upon
or disposition of a particular matter as applied to a specific set of facts
involved does not render the same a rule.* . . .

5. "Rule" . . . does not include . . . action or inaction of an agency . . .
which . . .

(b) Is a decision or order in a contested case;

(c) Is an order which is directed to a specifically named person or to a
group of specifically named persons which does not constitute a general
class, and the order is served on the person or persons to whom it is
directed by the appropriate means applicable thereto. *The fact that the
named person who is being regulated serves a group of unnamed persons who will be affected does not make such order a "rule"* . . . [italics
supplied].[23]

Not only does the Wisconsin act retain the positive features of the
definition of a rule found in other acts and in the Model State Administrative Procedure Act,[24] but in effect it attempts to distinguish
clearly between rule making and adjudication. Moreover, the itali-
cized portions of 4 and 5 (c), above, make it clear that agency determinations of rates and similar decisions directed to specific parties,
though perhaps containing policy statements or indirectly affecting
general classes of unnamed persons, are not to be considered as rule
making; they are, rather, adjudicatory in character. On the other
hand, references in the federal act to "particular applicability" and

[23] Wis. Stat., sec. 227.01 (1955). Compare the American Bar Association's pro-
posed Administrative Code, which would include rate making within adjudication.
S. 1070, 86th Cong., 2d sess. For recent British reform experience, see Geoffrey
Marshall, "The Franks Committee on Administrative Tribunals and Enquiries,"
Public Administration, XXXV (Winter 1957), 347-58, and his "Tribunals and En-
quiries: Developments Since the Franks Report," *Public Administration,* XXXVI
(Autumn 1958), 261-70.

[24] " 'Rule' includes every regulation, standard, or statement of policy or interpretation of general application and future effect, including the amendment or
repeal thereof, adopted by an agency, whether with or without prior hearing, to
implement or make specific the law enforced or administered by it or to govern
its organization or procedure, but does not include regulations concerning only
the internal management of the agency and not directly affecting the rights of or
procedures available to the public" (Model State Administrative Procedure Act,
1946 *Handbook of the National Conference of Commissioners on Uniform State
Laws,* pp. 202-17, sec. 1[2]).

to the fixing of wages, rates, prices, and other specifics, as constituting rule making, serve to reinforce the already too apparent tendency to regard administrative policy making as properly judicial in character.

Were these specifics, which are almost always adversary in nature, removed from rule making and subjected to distinguishable minimal procedural requirements more proper for such proceedings, then the "gray" area would be reduced and administrators could more readily distinguish when they are "legislating" from when they are adjudicating. They could be free from having to abide with rigid procedural requirements common to adjudicatory proceedings when considering matters of general policy. And Congress could distinguish, too, by devising remedies appropriate respectively to rule making and adjudication in its attempt to fix upon public officers responsibility for ethical and effective conduct.[25]

Two other problems remain to be considered. These relate (1) to policies that may tend to discriminate against certain segments of the public, and (2) to the behavior of employees responsible for the application or enforcement of agency policies.

DISCRIMINATION

Most forms used by administrative agencies relate to applications, reports, records, or bonds. Many agencies require that various forms be completed as prerequisites for administrative consideration of ac-

25 The American Bar Association's proposed Agency Hearing Standards of Conduct Act would make it unlawful for any person to communicate ex parte with any agency member or hearing officer concerning any adjudicatory proceeding unless reasonable notice is given to all parties of record. All ex parte communications must be made a matter of record. S. 2374, 86th Cong., 1st sess. In his special message to Congress concerning off-the-record contacts, President Kennedy said: "This is a problem which can best be resolved in the context of the particular responsibilities and activities of each agency. I therefore recommend that the Congress enact legislation requiring each agency, within 120 days, to promulgate a code of behavior governing ex parte contacts within the agency, specifying the particular standard to be applied in each type of agency proceeding, and containing an absolute prohibition against ex parte contact in all proceedings between private parties in which law or agency regulation requires that a decision be made solely on the record of a formal hearing" (*New York Times*, April 28, 1961, p. 16).

tion sought by applicants. Usually, the action involves some benefit or other type of agency consent. Accordingly, forms constitute agency information and occasionally contain statements of general policy or otherwise add to statutory requirements.

It is elementary to a proper concept of equity or justice that agency policies, including those made known by forms, should not be discriminatory in their terms or application. In Wisconsin, an attempt has been made to preclude discriminatory administrative policies by both executive and legislative action. In 1954, Wisconsin's governor addressed the following letter to the heads of all state departments and agencies:

> It has been brought to my attention that a relatively small number of State of Wisconsin administrative agencies now use forms which require designations of race, color, nationality, religion, or similar references. I raise the question to you whether these designations accord with the letter and spirit of the law.
>
> In only one instance is an agency authorized by statute to require such information. Members of the public are likely to gain the impression, nevertheless, that all administrative requirements of this kind have the force of law.
>
> I believe it to be appropriate, therefore, that each state administrative agency evaluate any form designations of race, color, nationality, religion or similar references, which they now use, decide whether they should be retained, and communicate such decision therefor to this office.[26]

Only one Wisconsin statute authorized such a form designation, to be used for motor vehicle operators' licenses. In 1955, the Wisconsin legislature included in its revision of the state general administrative procedure act this provision:

> No rule, either in its terms or in its application, shall discriminate for or against any person by reason of his race, creed, color, national origin, or ancestry. Every person affected by a rule shall be entitled to the same benefits and subject to the same obligations as any other person under the same or similar circumstances.[27]

[26] Letter from Walter J. Kohler, Governor of Wisconsin, dated July 30, 1954, mimeographed, in the files of the Executive Office of the State of Wisconsin, State Capitol, Madison, Wisconsin.
[27] Wis. Stat., sec. 227.033 (1955).

The Wisconsin act defines forms as constituting rules.[28] The governor's letter had served to eliminate all such form designations except some required by four agencies. The legislature's action effected deletion of the remaining designations with the exception of the one required by statute on the motor vehicle operator's license form. Subsequently, this sole exception was repealed by separate statutory action. Throughout this process, the Wisconsin Governor's Commission on Human Rights pressured agencies to eliminate the form designations. It is also worth noting that the state's interest in this problem was initiated by the University of Wisconsin chapter of the National Association for the Advancement of Colored People.[29]

One other state, Michigan, has seen fit to include in its administrative procedure act a similar section forbidding discrimination by rule.[30] It is doubtful that such provisions add substantively to the Fourteenth Amendment or to the constitutional provisions of most states pertaining to equality. There seems as much justification, however, for legislative declaration in favor of the principle of equal treatment in rule making as in other fields.

ENFORCEMENT

Many complaints registered against public administration are responses to objectionable enforcement methods rather than to the content of agency policies. Inspectors and other enforcement personnel are often criticized for allegedly arbitrary, officious, or undiplomatic conduct.

Most enforcement of agency policies is successfully attained by use of educational methods as distinguished from coercion or the threat of adversary proceedings. Public administrators are usually cognizant of the importance of tact and discreet behavior in enforcement matters, and many agencies subject enforcement personnel to

[28] "A form which imposes requirements which are within the definition of a rule shall be treated as a rule . . ." (Wis. Stat., sec. 227.013 [1955]).

[29] The pertinent materials are in the files of the Governor's Commission on Human Rights of the State of Wisconsin, State Capitol, Madison, Wisconsin.

[30] Mich. Stat. Ann., sec. 3.560 (14a) (1952).

in-service training programs that stress methods short of coercion. Moreover, instruction manuals elaborate such procedures to guide personnel in applying agency policies to specific situations.

In spite of the widespread recognition in public administration of the efficacy of education in the achievement of enforcement objectives, complaints still occur. Two reasons appear accountable. First, enforcement personnel are often relatively undercompensated and undereducated. Second, civil service regulations make it difficult to terminate the employment of tactless or overly officious enforcement personnel.[31]

There is a correlation between effective human relations in administration, including tact and diplomacy, and the educational qualifications of enforcement personnel. The obvious remedy here is for government to compensate such personnel at a level high enough to attract well-qualified persons and to keep them in such positions. At the same time, civil service regulations should be made to accord with a true merit system by permitting easier removal of personnel who prove undesirable. Caution is necessary lest timid enforcement replace tactless enforcement. But it is clear that in many jurisdictions "civil service" and "merit" systems are not synonymous for the reason that civil service maintains a closed back door. This door must be opened if public administration is to advance much further along the road toward professionalization of, and public respect for, the public service.

[31] See, for example, Wisconsin Legislative Council, *1955 Report, Administrative Rule Making*, p. 203. For discussion of British regulations that are difficult for the layman to understand and comply with, see J. B. W. Armstrong, "Enforcement of Technical Regulations," *Public Administration*, XXVIII (Summer 1950), 103-8.

Chapter Six

*External
Controls*

Various legalistic controls have been devised and imposed by legislatures from time to time to limit discretion in administrative policy making. Judicial review has long been available as a check on administrative action, and it was the primary check until the last twenty-five years. Therefore, as agitation for reform of the administrative process reached a peak during the 1930's, it was natural that proposals for new controls were patterned after traditional judicial safeguards. Various proposals for administrative courts were made during this period. And the assumed success of the declaratory judgment proceeding prompted introduction of the declaratory ruling device into administrative law. This chapter evaluates these and some of the other legalistic controls of policy-making discretion in public administration.

JUDICIAL REVIEW

Judicial review is the traditional method of control to assure that administrative action is kept within legal bounds. Probably no area of administrative law is so complex or has received so much attention and analysis in legal writings as that relating to judicial review. The purpose here is not to enquire into each of its components, but merely to analyze some of the major features of this field of law so that certain tentative improvements may be suggested.

Declaratory judgment proceedings. The Conference of Commissioners on Uniform State Laws included in its Model State Administrative Procedure Act provision for judicial review of administrative rules in declaratory judgment proceedings. The conference reasoned that "certain impediments including the judicial requirement of an actual case or controversy and the doctrine of prior resort to administrative remedies have developed to prevent . . . [the declaratory judgment proceeding] . . . from having the general utility that is to be desired."[1]

The case made for the declaratory judgment proceeding in administrative law rests on its speed, economy, and efficiency and on the facts that it enables disputes to be determined in their incipiency, that court determination of the validity of an agency policy can be obtained without risking its violation, that it puts administrators on notice of the bounds of legality not to be transcended, and that such a proceeding supersedes archaic common-law writs.

Argument against the declaratory judgment proceeding stresses that prior resort to administrative proceedings is not required to procure a declaratory judgment. Moot or hypothetical questions might therefore be forthcoming, and under circumstances adverse to the agency.

Little information, moreover, is available concerning how much the declaratory judgment proceeding, where permitted, is utilized. Because such proceeding is made available only by statutory law, and because many courts hold to the doctrine that statutory law in derogation of the common law shall be strictly construed, it is doubtful that the declaratory judgment can be said to supersede common-law writs. Indeed, there is nothing in the notes to drafts of the Model Act to indicate that the Act's creators intended the petition for declaratory judgment to be the exclusive method of obtaining judicial re-

[1] *1943 Handbook of the National Conference of Commissioners on Uniform State Laws*, pp. 235-36.

view of administrative rules. Accordingly, common-law writs for judicial review merit analysis.

Common-law writs. The validity of an administrative decision relating to a particular person sometimes depends on the validity of the underlying administrative policy or rule. The traditional method of obtaining review in such cases is by one of the so-called common-law extraordinary writs—certiorari, mandamus, prohibition, habeas corpus, and quo warranto.

Many writers have been highly critical of these remedies on the ground that the decision in a case frequently turns on the correctness of the remedy sought rather than on the merits. It is often difficult for an attorney to determine the proper remedy in a given case. As indicated in Chapter 4, mandamus is usually held an improper remedy when a "discretionary" act is involved. Certiorari and prohibition are generally improper unless the action to be reviewed is of a "judicial or quasi-judicial" nature, and thus they would not be adequate for review of administrative policies or rules. And habeas corpus and quo warranto writs have very restricted application so far as review of administrative action is concerned. It is safe to conclude, therefore, that the common-law extraordinary writs do not offer much assurance of obtaining judicial review of administrative policies.[2]

Other proceedings. Judicial review of agency policy is sometimes obtained through an action to restrain the enforcement of a rule. The validity of policies is occasionally determined in actions brought by or on behalf of agencies to enforce rules or to impose penalties for noncompliance with rules. Statutory injunction proceedings are available for the enforcement of some agency rules, and the validity of agency policies may be determined in such proceedings. Decisions in actions between private parties occasionally depend on the validity of administrative policies. An issue of negligence, for example, may turn on whether the defendant complied with a safety rule of an administrative agency and, furthermore, whether the rule in question is valid.

Clear legislation needed. When a legislature, by statute, permits

[2] See, for example, Davis, *Administrative Law and Government* (1960), pp. 377-83.

resort to declaratory judgment proceedings for judicial review of administrative policies, it should make clear whether it intends such proceedings to be the exclusive means of obtaining such review or whether the other methods discussed are permissible. Preferably, the legislature should either specify the forms of proceedings available or provide that review may be had in any type of proceeding where the issue of a rule's validity is material. This would eliminate much of the confusion concerning the availability of various proceedings for obtaining judicial review of agency policies.

Scope of judicial review. Many articles have been written on the scope of judicial review of administrative action, but very few distinguish between review of adjudicatory decisions and review of other agency action. In prescribing review, a legislature should adhere to a distinction by making voidable an adjudicatory decision unsupported by evidence in the record submitted. No comparable provision for review of other agency action, including agency policies or rules, should obtain, for usually a policy is not based on any official record of hearing or fact finding. As discussed in Chapter 4, the presumption of validity or reasonableness should attach alike to administrative rules and legislative enactments.

Political scientists hesitate in accepting the all-or-nothing approach of lawyers that all administrative action consists either of rule making or adjudication. Plainly, much administrative action does not fit this dichotomy. Nevertheless, for judicial review purposes, there is propriety in distinguishing adjudication from all other administrative action. The Federal Administrative Procedure Act, though it lumps rule making and adjudication together for most judicial review purposes, provides that an agency action may be held invalid if "unsupported by substantial evidence" only when the action has been subject to formal hearing procedures.[3] The only other jurisdictions with provisions in their general administrative procedure statutes dealing with the scope of judicial review of ad-

3 60 U. S. Stat. 237, sec. 10 (e) (1946). For discussion of proposals to change this formula, see Ralph F. Fuchs, "The Proposed New Code of Administrative Procedure," *Ohio State Law Journal*, XIX (Spring 1958), 422-31, at p. 429.

ministrative rules are Arizona, California, North Carolina, Ohio, Virginia, and Wisconsin. The relevant statutory provisions of all but Ohio are similar to the federal act, though less specific. Only Ohio provides that rules may be held void if they are "unreasonable" or unlawful.[4]

Interpretative rules and retroactivity.   That courts, by their action, often distinguish between "interpretative" and "legislative" rules is reasonably clear. But the distinction is a fuzzy one. There is no need to probe deeply into the pertinent law here.[5] Suffice it to point out that every administrative agency is generally considered to have inherent powers to interpret the legislative provisions it administers. Since in theory agencies are merely finding the intent of the legislature when they make interpretative rules, courts reserve the right to substitute their judgment for that of the agencies on the correctness of such rules. On the other hand, courts seldom question the correctness of policy expressed in so-called "legislative" rules—that is, substantive agency policies that apply, fill in the details of, or make more specific statutory standards of delegation—so long as agencies do not exceeed their legal authority.

Retroactivity is the most frequently criticized feature of judicial review of interpretative rules. The reasoning is that if an agency is caused by judicial disapproval of an interpretative rule to adopt a new interpretative rule, the latter operates retroactively because, like a judicial decision that construes a statute, the new rule merely purports to declare what the statute has always meant. Accordingly, past agency action under the voided rule is, by implication, made invalid.

The fact that the distinction between an interpretative and a legislative rule is often an arbitrary and difficult one further aggravates the confusion in the law that retroactivity creates. It is true that

4 Ariz. Laws, ch. 97, sec. 11 (1952); 1951 Calif. Gov't. Code and 1953 Supplement, sec. 11440; N. Car. Stat., sec. 150-32 (1953 Supplement); Ohio Code Ann., sec. 154-72 (Page, 1946); Va. Code Ann., sec. 9-6.9 (1952 Supplement); Wis. Stat., sec. 227.05 (1955).

5 For an authoritative discussion of this matter, see Kenneth C. Davis, *Administrative Law Treatise* (St. Paul, Minn.: West Publishing Co., 1958), Chapter 5.

the problem is alleviated considerably by the disposition of courts to presume the correctness of an interpretative rule if it was made contemporaneously with the statute it interprets, if it is of long standing, or if the statute was re-enacted while the rule was in existence. Nevertheless, it would be desirable for legislatures to provide by statute that agency action taken pursuant to an administrative rule shall not be affected by a change in that rule, whether such change is effected by agency or court action.

Availability of judicial review. The timing of a request for judicial review of an administrative rule may affect the availability of judicial review. The question of timing is commonly treated in reference to the doctrine of "exhaustion of administrative remedies." Various reasons have been advanced to support the exhaustion doctrine, the foremost of which, perhaps, is that it facilitates orderly procedure and avoids the delay and confusion that would result if a case could be shifted back and forth between the court and agency at every stage of a proceeding. Though the exhaustion doctrine developed as a doctrine of judicial self-limitation and is frequently applied by courts, it does not operate without exceptions. In general, it is disregarded if exhaustion of administrative remedies would result in irreparable injury or if the administrative remedy is inadequate—as, for example, when the operating statute under which the agency is acting is unconstitutional.

Judicial review is occasionally denied for the reason that the person requesting review has no standing to challenge the policy or administrative action in question. Such decisions usually refer to an absence of "legal right" or an absence of a "case or controversy." Though the concept of "legal right" defies exact definition, courts properly give weight to such factors as the directness and magnitude of the injury or threatened injury, the legislative policy of reviewability, if any, and the agency's judgment as to whether the petitioner is sufficiently "interested" to permit him to intervene in the proceedings before the agency. The basic question is whether the petitioner asserts an interest deserving legal protection under the circumstances. Answers to this question vary from case to case.

Considerable case law, developed in federal courts, demonstrates that some actions of administrative agencies are nonreviewable, such as an agency's exercise of, or failure to exercise, its prosecuting power and certain actions conferring or refusing to confer special benefits. However, the doctrine of nonreviewability is seldom invoked in connection with administrative rules.

So long as any administrative rule may be judicially reviewed—if the time of the request for review is proper, if the petitioner has standing to challenge, and if the exhaustion of remedies doctrine is not applied arbitrarily—then the law pertaining to judicial review would appear satisfactory. The law concerning who has the right to challenge the validity of administrative rules is largely court law, and, therefore, there is probably little that a legislature can do to improve the "legal rights" formula.[6]

DECLARATORY RULINGS

Unlike external controls, declaratory rulings do not operate independently of the administrative agency, for their effectiveness is dependent upon the willingness of the agency itself to issue them. They are included in this discussion because they serve to limit administrative discretion in the application or enforcement of administrative policies. Declaratory rulings, moreover, are analogous to declaratory judgments because they provide a means of determining the course of administrative action at an earlier stage than otherwise would be possible.

Provisions for declaratory rulings are included in Wisconsin's Administrative Procedure Act, the Model State Administrative Procedure Act, and the Federal Administrative Procedure Act.[7] Both the

6 Nevertheless, several proposals for legislation would facilitate judicial intervention in administrative proceedings prior to exhaustion of administrative remedies. See Heady, "The New Reform Movement in Regulatory Administration," pp. 89-100, at p. 97.

7 Wis. Stat., sec. 227.06 (1955); "Model Act," sec. 7, in *1946 Handbook of the National Conference of Commissioners on Uniform State Laws*, pp. 202-17; 60 U. S. Stat. 237, sec. 5 (d) (1946).

majority and minority views expressed in the report of the Attorney General's Committee on Administrative Procedure recommended that provisions authorizing declaratory rulings be included in administrative procedure legislation.[8]

The basic purpose of declaratory ruling procedures is to accomplish in administrative law what declaratory judgment procedures have accomplished in other fields of law. The common objective of both types of procedure is preventive—to enable a person to ascertain prior to embarking on a course of action whether such action would violate the law. The expense of trial and error is thereby avoided.[9]

The need for the declaratory ruling device apparently emanated from certain experiences in the field of federal taxation. In some instances, taxpayers lost considerable sums because they entered into transactions based on interpretative rules that subsequently were held void and hence were changed with retroactive effect.[10]

Some writers have attributed a disadvantage or limitation to the declaratory ruling procedure. Where the issuance of rulings is discretionary, the effectiveness of the device is dependent on the agency's attitude toward it. Some writers have argued that issuance ought to be mandatory, but most contend that, for a number of reasons, it should be discretionary. For one thing, administrators may be doubtful about the correct interpretation of the law and would be reluctant to issue declaratory rulings by which they feel bound. For another, their success requires that the critical facts will not be altered by subsequent events. If these facts are altered after a ruling, the agency may feel impelled to disregard its ruling, and then litigation will be in the offing. And there is always the possibility that a person may abuse the device by seeking successive rulings on slightly altered facts

---

[8] Committee on Administrative Procedure, *Final Report of the Attorney General's Committee on Administrative Procedure*, pp. 30-33, 231.

[9] Davis, *Administrative Law and Government* (1960), pp. 109-11.

[10] Herman Oliphant, "Declaratory Rulings," *American Bar Association Journal*, XXIV (1938), 7-9; Walter Gellhorn, *Administrative Law: Cases and Comments* (Brooklyn, 1947), pp. 804-6. For discussion of the possible uses and abuses of declaratory rulings, see Walter Gellhorn, "Declaratory Rulings by Federal Agencies," *Annals of the American Academy of Political and Social Science*, CCXXI (1942), 153-59.

in an effort to reach the outer limits of legal conduct, thereby unduly taxing the resources of the agency.

Though the declaratory ruling procedure is utilized infrequently, there is no indication that it has worked unsatisfactorily. Though agencies ought to retain discretion whether to issue rulings in particular cases, legislatures could provide, as some state legislatures do, that a petition for a ruling must either be denied in writing, with the stated reasons therefor, or be scheduled for hearing within a reasonable time.[11] Such a legislative requirement tends to ensure that each petition is given fair consideration without, at the same time, depriving the agency of its discretion.

ADMINISTRATIVE COURTS

Administrative courts, as commonly understood, may vary widely in type from agency "adjudication boards," or boards of appeal, to courts enjoying substantially the same status as so-called "constitutional courts." Yet certain underlying propositions are common to most proposals for the establishment of administrative courts. The primary ones are: (1) that adjudicative functions should be separated from prosecuting and legislative functions; and (2) that there should be liberal judicial review of administrative action, extending to review of facts as well as law and sometimes even to trial *de novo*.

It has been argued that administrative courts would democratize the administrative process by assuring a fair hearing for the party affected by administrative action. Violation of the principles of "natural justice" and separation of powers is contended when an administrator acts in his own cause. It is emphasized that often an administrative agency will adopt a policy, investigate its alleged violation, prosecute for its alleged violation, and finally sit in judgment on the question whether it has been violated. Fairness can only be assured, it is claimed, if the judicial part of the process is separated from the legislative and prosecuting functions as permitted by an administrative court system.

11 See, for example, Wis. Stat., sec. 227.06 (4) (1955).

Arguments in favor of administrative courts, always a controversial subject, have evoked rebuttal. Most administrative court proposals have not met with much success in the United States.[12]

Opponents of administrative courts view the administrative process as composed of interrelated and inherent functions. And the fact that some of these functions resemble legislating and prosecuting while others resemble adjudicating does not, in their view, justify vesting the adjudicative function in a body independent of the agency. Judicial review is already a long and tedious process, they reason, and the division of responsibility occasioned by independent adjudication boards or administrative courts would only create more confusion and delay. Speed and efficiency would be sacrificed even though they are among the primary reasons for resort to the administrative process in the first instance. Insofar as fairness may commend a separation of functions, it is argued, this can be achieved more efficiently by internal separation of functions or by special hearing officers than by special administrative courts.[13]

The liberalized judicial review of administrative action generally contemplated by proponents of administrative courts extends to a trial *de novo* on the facts. This position stresses that everyone affected by administrative action should have a right to a trial *de novo* by an "impartial" tribunal. Opponents claim that this is based on two false assumptions: (1) that there is such a thing as one true find-

[12] But the administrative court idea was revived in 1955; see *Report of the Task Force on Legal Services and Procedure of the Commission on Organization of the Executive Branch of the Government* (Second Hoover Commission) (Washington, D. C.: U. S. Gov't. Printing Office, 1955), pp. 241-46. See also the recommendation of the Second Hoover Commission to establish an administrative court with three sections: a tax section (to replace the U. S. Tax Court); a trade section (to replace trade regulation exercised by the FTC, ICC, FCC, CAB, FRB, FCP, and the Tariff Commission); and a labor section (which would pre-empt the NLRB's jurisdiction involving unfair labor practices). In 1957, Senator Alexander Smith introduced a bill to create such a court: S. 2292, 85th Cong., 1st sess. (1957).

[13] For discussions opposing recent proposals for administrative courts, see Robert W. Minor, "The Administrative Court, Variations on a Theme," *Ohio State Law Journal*, XIX (Spring 1958), 380-99; Heady, "The New Reform Movement in Regulatory Administration"; Auerbach, "Should Administrative Agencies Perform Adjudicatory Functions?" *Wisconsin Law Review* (1959), pp. 95-116.

ing of fact; and (2) that judicially trained persons are inherently more adept at finding the true facts than administrative officials.

From a rationale that the power over a man's subsistence is a power over his will, and that lifetime tenure is therefore essential to an impartial judiciary, some administrative court bills have provided for unlimited security of tenure for the judges. Those opposed to administrative courts reply that impartiality is not always a characteristic of the judiciary and, furthermore, that it would be undesirable to have judges entrenched in the administrative system who might be unsympathetic or unresponsive to the programs of the administration in power.

Administrative court proposals are sometimes supported as a means of relieving existing court congestion and thereby expediting the settlement of disputes involving administrative agencies. Opponents answer that it would be more economical simply to reform the present court system.

It is also argued in support of administrative courts that judges would be able to specialize and attain the expertness necessary for understanding many problems in administrative law. Opponents respond that such problems are no more technical or difficult than other legal problems and, in any event, insofar as expertness may be required, it can be developed better in administrative agencies than in administrative courts.

Many of the arguments for administrative courts were expressly or implicitly advanced in the celebrated "Hector Memorandum" affair. On the occasion of his resignation as a member of the Civil Aeronautics Board in 1959, Louis J. Hector wrote a controversial memorandum to the President which amounted to one of the most comprehensive and formidable attacks ever made against federal regulatory commissions. The board's response was equally extreme in its opposition to administrative courts generally and to Hector's recommendations and criticisms of the CAB specifically.[14] So con-

14 In his letter of resignation to the President, dated September 10, 1959, Hector wrote: ". . . The CAB is a creature imprisoned by its own structure and procedures. It is unable to form clear policy. . . . It is unable to administer its affairs with

tentious did controversies concerning the various independent commissions become in the late 1950's that President Kennedy felt it necessary, within a day after his election, to ask James M. Landis to study these matters and report to him.[15]

Dispassionate observers generally agree that the arguments for and against administrative court proposals are both somewhat extreme and exaggerated, and they tend to view such controversies as that between Hector and the CAB in this light. They point out, for example, that the idea of separation of legislative and prosecuting functions from adjudicative functions may have merit in certain situations, but that if this idea were implemented too broadly or carried to its logical conclusion the results would probably be unfortunate. Separation of prosecuting and adjudicative functions might be desirable, certain circumstances permitting, in agencies dealing with questions involving the possibility of revocation of important licenses, while separation might be manifestly undesirable in agencies concerned with the settlement of small claims where the administrator may be as much interested in expeditiously giving a claimant what he deserves as the claimant is in receiving it.

---

vigor and dispatch. . . . The policies and plans of the CAB are not coordinated with those of other agencies. . . . The problems of the CAB are not transitory or superficial. They are basic. In my opinion, they are born of the very concept of an independent administrative commission." Among possible remedies, Hector proposed transfer of judicial and appellate duties of the CAB to a "true" administrative court "free from policy making or administrative detail," the members of which should be appointed for a fixed term and be "as genuinely independent as judges of the statutory courts . . ." (Louis J. Hector, "Memorandum to the President, Problems of the CAB and the Independent Regulatory Commissions," as printed in *Independent Regulatory Agencies Legislation*, Hearings before the Committee on Interstate and Foreign Commerce, House of Representatives, 86th Cong., 2d sess., March 15, 16, 18, 22, 23, 25, 29, 30, 31, April 1, 4, 7, and 8, 1960, pp. 336-411, at pp. 337, 338, 405). The board's lengthy response is printed as "Comments on the Hector Memorandum," prepared by General Counsel and Adopted by the Civil Aeronautics Board, *ibid.*, pp. 412-507.

15 When James M. Landis reported to John F. Kennedy, then President-elect, his sweeping indictment of regulatory commissions was almost as condemning as Hector's charges, but Landis proposed different solutions. His criticisms of the commissions included, apart from their faulty organization without leadership, their failure to do forward planning, their susceptibility to ex parte representation, their need for better personnel, their concern for time-wasting and costly trivia as against broad policy, and their failure to establish criteria for case-by-case de-

Whether to have administrative courts or boards of appeal to review application of administrative policies and other agency action is a highly controversial topic. No state at present has an administrative court with jurisdiction to hear appeals from all state administrative agencies. Were such courts established, they might encounter constitutional difficulties in some jurisdictions as being in conflict with the so-called "constitutional courts."

"PRENATAL" CLEARANCE AND REVIEW

Judicial review operates to ensure the legality of agency policies only after a policy has been put into effect. At best a minimal protection of the public interest, judicial review may be invoked only if someone has the time and money to utilize this method of challenging a policy he believes to be illegal. Accordingly, various proposals to provide what might be termed "prenatal" clearance and review have gained popularity in recent years.

Clearance by attorney general. Prenatal review usually takes the form of submission of proposed administrative rules to the jurisdiction's attorney general for approval as to their legality. At least ten states now have provisions of this nature in their general administra-

cisions. On this last point, for example, he reported of the FCC: "In broadcast license cases no criteria for decision have evolved. . . . No firm decisional policy has evolved from these case-by-case dispositions. Instead the anonymous opinion writers for the commission pick from a collection of standards those that will support whatever decision the commission chooses to make." Instead of recommending the creation of administrative courts, Landis proposed: strengthening the powers of the President to reorganize the commissions, with their chairmen to serve at the pleasure of the President; creating within the Executive Office of the President three top staff offices to coordinate and develop transportation policy, communications policy, and energy policy, respectively, and a fourth office to exercise oversight of regulatory agencies; and creating a permanent administrative conference, the secretariat of which would assume the functions now exercised by the Office of Administrative Procedure within the Department of Justice as well as those exercised by the Civil Service Commission with respect to the qualifications and grading of hearing examiners. He recommended, furthermore, that the President "issue an executive order dealing with the ethics of Government employes and their duty to reject and refrain from receiving ex parte presentations in pending matters before them for adjudication on the records" (Landis, *Report on Regulatory Agencies to the President-Elect,* pp. 53, 83-87.) For the President's response, see *supra,* Chapter 5, note 13, page 120, and note 25, page 127.

tive procedure acts: Connecticut, Indiana, Iowa, Maryland, Michigan, Minnesota, Nebraska, North Dakota, Pennsylvania, and Tennessee.[16] Most of the provisions are quite general. Connecticut and Nebraska do not even restrict review by the attorney general to legality. The acts of the other eight states specify either "legality" or "form and legality."

None of the acts include criteria, standards, or factors that should be considered by the attorney general in determining the legality or illegality of a proposed rule. In other words, the scope of review is not specified. Most of the statutes merely provide that a rule is not valid until it has been approved by the attorney general as to legality. However, the Pennsylvania act stipulates that failure of the agency to submit a rule to the attorney general shall not invalidate the rule, and the Nebraska act provides, in effect, that the opinion of the attorney general shall be advisory only, except with respect to rules of the Nebraska Railway Commission.

Clearance of proposed agency rules by the attorney general has certain apparent advantages. The agency benefits in that clearance tends to assure it that its rules will be valid and capable of withstanding attack in the courts. This is especially important to the agency with respect to controversial rules. The attorney general gains an advantage in being able to check on the validity of a rule while it is in its formative stage, for ultimately he may be responsible for defending the rule in court. Finally, those affected by agency rules are relieved of the burden of either complying with unlawful rules or contesting their validity in court.

Nevertheless, clearance by the attorney general has been criticized, chiefly on the grounds that the procedure is subject to abuse. It has been suggested, for example, that an attorney general who dislikes the substance of a proposed rule might camouflage his bias in the

---

[16] Conn. Stat., sec. 282 (1949); Ind. Stat. Ann., sec. 60-1505 (Burns, 1951); Iowa Code Ann., sec. 17A.2 (1953 Supplement); Md. Code Ann., Art. 41, sec. 9 (1951); Mich. Comp. Laws, sec. 27.74 (1949); Minn. Stat., sec. 15.042 (4) (1953); Neb. Stat., sec. 84-905.01 (1943; Reissue of 1950); N. Dak. Code, sec. 28-3202 (1943); Pa. Stat. Ann., Tit. 71, sec. 7110.21 (Purdon, 1953 Supplement); Tenn. Code Ann., sec. 1034.21 (Williams, 1934; 1943 Replacement).

guise of determining that the rule would be held invalid if adopted. The possibility of such abuse is allegedly enhanced by the fact that an attorney general's decision to disapprove a rule proposal apparently would not be subject to judicial review in the absence of special legislation providing for such review.[17] Another, less serious, objection to this type of prenatal review is that it is time-consuming. The practice of voluntary submission engaged in by some state agencies in Wisconsin seems to have worked satisfactorily.[18] A possible compromise might take the form of a provision similar to the one included in the Nebraska act. The latter makes the attorney general's opinion advisory only but requires him to report to each legislative session any existing rules that he believes to be invalid.

If a legislature is impelled to require the clearance of rule proposals with the attorney general and thus to give him life and death powers over such agency policy proposals, then safeguards against possible abuse should be included in the legislation establishing such a procedure. Emergency rules should be excepted from the procedure. A limited period should be specified within which the attorney general must act on rule proposals submitted to him. The limits of his powers of review should be spelled out in far greater detail than mere reference to "legality" affords. He should be required to explain in writing to the agency his reasons for disapproving a proposal. And, finally, the agency should have the opportunity to secure judicial review of his decisions.

[17] The fear of abuse has some foundation in experience. In Michigan, disapproval of a rule has occasionally hinged on substantive provisions of the rule rather than on its form or legality. Morever, the Michigan attorney general has added to statutory clearance requirement by requiring an agency, for example, to adopt a rule before and after his approval of the rule, though not required by statute, and he will not permit a rule to paraphrase a statute, though not prohibited by statute. It is also reported that the attorney general's office in Michigan has not given uniformity of treatment to all agencies. Not only have some agencies been given favored treatment, but treatment has varied as between the assistants in the attorney general's office. As a result, agencies attempt to secure review by those assistants who have acquired a reputation of being favorably disposed to agency rules (Heady, *Administrative Procedure Legislation in the States*, pp. 49-54). See also Note, "Veto of Agency Rules," *Drake Law Review*, II (1952), 35-38.

[18] Wisconsin Legislative Council, *1955 Report, Administrative Rule Making*, pp. 138-39.

Legislative clearance and review.   In recent years, some state legis-latures have attempted to control administrative rule making by providing that the legislature may invalidate rules already in effect. Between 1953 and 1955, Wisconsin's administrative procedure act contained a provision authorizing the legislature to invalidate any existing rule by joint resolution.[19] The administrative procedure acts of five other states—Connecticut, Kansas, Michigan, Nebraska, and Virginia—contain similar legislative review provisions.[20]

None of these provisions requires that the rules be approved by the legislature before they can become effective. Connecticut, Michigan, and Nebraska, however, provide for the submission of all rules prior to each legislative session either to the legislature or to a legislative committee for consideration. The Kansas and Virginia acts do not establish any such procedure, and consequently agency rules in these states will not be subjected to legislative scrutiny unless some inter-ested person takes it upon himself to request legislative review. All five states provide either expressly or by implication that a rule dis-approved by the legislature is void.

A requirement that all rules must be approved by the legislature theoretically gives the legislature a very complete and direct control over the administration of the laws it has enacted. In practice, how-ever, such a requirement would probably mean that approval would be merely perfunctory or that the legislature would become bogged down in detail; it would thereby defeat one of the main purposes of delegation. Wisconsin's limited experience with a requirement that rules pertaining to food standards be approved by the legislature before they become effective tends to support this conclusion.[21] In view of the fact that the typical state legislature meets only bien-nially and few legislatures meet for more than several months each year, a clearance requirement probably would also result in too great

[19] Wis. Laws, Chapter 331 (1953).

[20] Conn. Stat., sec. 285 (1949); Kans. Stat., sec. 77-410 (Corrick, 1949); Mich. Comp. Laws, sec. 27.78b (1948); Neb. Stat., sec. 84-904 (1943; Reissue of 1950), as amended by Neb. Laws, Chap. 359 (1953); Va. Code Ann., sec. 9-6.9 (d) (1952 Supplement).

[21] Wisconsin Legislative Council, *1955 Report, Administrative Rule Making*, pp. 61-63.

a delay before many rules could be put into effect. A provision exempting emergency situations would seem to be needed, but such a provision would likely receive frequent use, perhaps to the point of being abused.

Thus, a procedure designed to have the legislature pass on all rules before they become effective has practical limitations and, if used, should be limited to selected fields of agency policy making where such specific legislative control is deemed to be of special importance. It would seem preferable to adopt a provision—similar to the one enacted by several states—that would authorize the legislature to invalidate an objectionable rule by joint resolution.

Legislative clearance and review procedures of this type, however, may present constitutional problems in some jurisdictions. Wisconsin's attorney general ruled in a 1954 opinion that the Wisconsin law authorizing the legislature to invalidate a rule by joint resolution was unconstitutional. He based his opinion on the constitutional provision that no law shall be enacted except by bill. Approximately half the states have similar provisions in their constitutions. According to the opinion, "any action the legislature takes that makes a change in or obliterates a departmental rule effects a change in the law," and such action must therefore be taken by bill, not by joint resolution.[22]

There is ample authority for the proposition that a constitutional provision requiring all laws to be enacted by bill means that a law cannot be enacted by joint resolution. The more doubtful point would seem to be whether the courts of each state that has this type of provision would consider administrative rules to constitute "law" within the meaning of the provision. This would appear to be a particularly significant question in those states where courts still pay "lip service" to the doctrine that delegation of power to administrative agencies to make rules is not the delegation of legislative power, but rather the delegation of power to "fill in the details" or to find facts. In any event, the constitutional problem merits consideration

22 Helstad and Boyer, "Legislative Controls of Administrative Rule Making," pp. 1,048-51, at p. 1,049.

whenever legislative clearance or review of administrative rules by means of the joint resolution is being proposed.

The 1955 revision of the Wisconsin administrative procedure act dropped the provision for repeal by joint resolution and created in its place a special joint legislative committee, consisting of two senators and three assemblymen, known as the Committee for Review of Administrative Rules. Although the committee has advisory powers only, it may hold public hearings, make investigations, subpoena witnesses, administer oaths, and, by majority vote, request that an agency hold a hearing. Members of the Wisconsin legislature had frequently voiced the need for better understanding between the legislature and administrative agencies, and between the agencies and the public, with respect to administrative rules. The committee was created to satisfy that need by providing a formal device for screening complaints concerning rule making and for channeling pertinent information and recommendations to the legislature.[23]

An earlier proposal made in Wisconsin, which was rejected, would have authorized such a committee to suspend any rule adopted after the adjournment of the previous legislative session, such suspension to remain in effect until the end of the following legislative session. This proposal would have enabled the legislature to act on all controversial rules prior to their taking effect. There was some objection to the proposal, however, on the grounds that it would vest too much authority in a few members of the legislature and that its constitutionality would be questionable.

Those in favor of legislative clearance or review procedures have cited certain advantages.[24] First, it is contended, such procedures

---

23 Wis. Stat., sec. 227.041 (1955).

24 Proponents often cite British experience of parliamentary control. See, for example, the following by Bernard Schwartz: "Legislative Control of Administrative Rules and Regulations: The American Experience," *New York University Law Review,* XXX (May 1955), 1,031-45; "The Administrative Process and Congressional Control," *Federal Bar Journal,* XVI (October-December 1956), 519-38; and "Legislative Oversight: Control of Administrative Agencies," *American Bar Association Journal,* XLIII (January 1957), 19-22. See also Note, "Legislative Control of Administrative Rules," *Columbia Law Review,* XLI (May 1941), 946-50; " 'Laying on the Table'—A Device for Legislative Control over Delegated Powers," *Harvard Law Review,* LXV (February 1952), 637-48; Robert W. Ginnane, "The

tend to give the legislature greater control over the administration of laws enacted by it, and, consequently, popular control over law-making is extended. This tends to bring administrative policy making into accord with constitutional theory. Second, it is argued, if administrators know that rules may be subjected to legislative scrutiny, they are likely to draft them more carefully with a view toward complying with legislative intent. Legislative clearance or review procedures therefore have a salutary effect on agency policy making that should redound to the benefit of legislators, administrative officials, and the public even without review procedures being invoked. Finally, it is reasoned, such procedures would tend to relieve administrators of the pressures for rule changes brought to bear by individual legislators on behalf of constituents. At the least, administrators would be able to point to established procedures as the proper means of obtaining changes in rules.[25]

After the various arguments are weighed, a requirement that the legislature must pass on all rules before they become effective appears to be incompatible with the very reasons for resort to the administrative process as discussed in the Introduction. The objective of popular control over administrative policy making, moreover, might well be hampered—rather than advanced—by such a clearance requirement with its attendant disadvantages of the burden of technical detail, less time for important legislative decisions, failure to act prior to adjournment, and the possibility that a legislative committee could preclude majority approval.

Control of Federal Administration by Congressional Resolutions and Committees," *Harvard Law Review*, LXVI (February 1953), 569-611; Frank C. Newman and Harry J. Keaton, "Congress and the Faithful Execution of Laws—Should Legislators Supervise Administrators?" *California Law Review*, XLI (Winter 1953), 565-95.

[25] Since 1944, the House of Commons has appointed at each session a Select Committee on Statutory Instruments, popularly known as the "Scrutinizing Committee," as a means of reinforcing its control over "delegated legislation." For appraisals of the functioning of this committee, see A. H. Hanson, "The Select Committee on Statutory Instruments, 1944-1949," *Public Administration*, XXVII (Winter 1949), 278-88; and F. A. Stacey, "The Select Committee on Statutory Instruments—A Reply to Mr. Hanson," *Public Administration*, XXVIII (Winter 1950), 333-35. For experience in Northern Ireland, see S. A. Walkland, "Parliamentary Control of Delegated Legislation in Northern Ireland," *Public Administration*, XXXVII (Autumn 1959), 257-65.

Worthy of emphasis is a disadvantage that applies to all devices that place burdens on administrative policy making. To escape such burdens, agencies are more likely to adopt rules in the guise of informal or unpublished policies. Michigan experience seems to give credence to this apprehension. Ninety Michigan agency rules were filed in 1945 prior to the imposition of clearance requirements for rules. By 1950, just three years after the imposition of clearance requirements, the figure had dropped to eighteen for all agencies.[26]

Most disadvantages or limitations of legislative clearance or review can be overcome if the legislature is merely given the power to invalidate rules by disapproval rather than required to approve rules before they become effective or to act on all rules adopted by agencies. The Michigan experience, however, indicates that the procedure suggested is subject to one drawback. Since a rule is given legislative consideration only when someone complains about the rule, the hearings take on the form of adversary proceedings, the complainant being one party and the agency the other. Because of the limited scope of such hearings, many facts that should enter into considerations of administrative policy making are likely to be omitted.

Executive clearance and review.   A requirement that agency rules be submitted to the chief executive for approval is a less popular means of controlling administrative policy making than approval by the attorney general or approval or review by the legislature. Only Indiana and Nebraska require that substantially all administrative rules be approved by the governor before they become effective.[27]

Many of the advantages and disadvantages discussed with respect to legislative clearance of rules are equally applicable to executive clearance. In theory, if not in practice, the latter would give the chief executive direct and extensive control over administrative policy making, just as legislative clearance would theoretically vest such con-

---

[26] The Michigan experience is discussed in Heady, *Administrative Procedure Legislation in the States*, pp. 54-62; and Glendon A. Schubert, "Legislative Adjudication of Administrative Legislation," *Journal of Public Law,* VII (Spring 1958), 135-61.

[27] Ind. Stat. Ann., sec. 60-1505 (Burns, 1951); Neb. Laws, Chap. 359, sec. 2 (1953).

trol in the legislature. Executive clearance is subject similarly to most of the shortcomings of legislative clearance, namely in the burden of detail imposed and in the possibilities for abuse presented. Clearance through the chief executive, nevertheless, has one advantage over legislative clearance: The chief executive's office functions continuously, whereas the legislature functions only intermittently.

It seems likely that the chief executive would have to surround himself with a substantial staff of experts in order to do a conscientious job of passing on the merits of all rule proposals of administrative agencies within his jurisdiction.

PART THREE
***
BUREAUCRACY
AND
DEMOCRACY

Chapter Seven

✳✳✳

Assuring
Public
Responsibility

If any theme can be drawn from this analysis of some of the major problems of the administrative process pertaining to agency policy making, it is that the need for administrative discretion may often run counter to the feasibility of imposing certain kinds of external controls on agencies. Moreover, where controls can reasonably be imposed, their effectiveness ultimately depends on the quality, integrity, and sense of public responsibility of administrative officers and personnel.

Fundamental to governmental responsibility in a democracy, nevertheless, is the concept of representative government which, if it is to prevail, requires an elective legislative body to contrive and exercise controls over appointed administrators and the administrative process. Ideally, this is expressed in terms of a government of law rather than a government of men.

A consistent motivating force behind all methods yet devised by legislatures to control administrative policy making is the argument that, in general, administrative agencies cannot be depended upon to exercise the responsibility necessary to assure that the ideal of a government of law shall prevail. To render such assurance it is necessary, therefore, for legislatures to limit administrative discretion in various ways.

Two faults in this argument are apparent. First, it presumes that legislatures have been highly successful in devising effective controls. Though the discussion of controls in the previous chapter indicates that each control has certain advantages, it is also noted that each has its shortcomings, limitations, and disadvantages, and that the cure is often more damaging than the disease it is intended to remedy. Secondly, the argument presumes that administrative agencies are the only organs of government in need of reform. Legislative, as well as administrative, behavior cannot remain static if the desired responsibility is to be realized.

Regardless of the number and types of controls devised by a legislature to govern administrative policy making, administrative responsibility will not necessarily follow. It seems quite clear, for example, that legislatures too frequently delegate policy-making discretion in broad, vague, and sometimes almost meaningless language. Administrators are thereby deprived of adequate legislative direction and clear standards that can serve as conclusive guides for the formulation of agency policies. It also seems quite clear that legislatures need to fashion new techniques to assure continuous improvement of the process of agency policy making, techniques that are free from many of the afflictions of the older devices and will not unduly fetter necessary administrative discretion or otherwise pervert the *raison d'être* of the administrative process.

Two broad remedies, as yet virtually untried or ignored, are suggested: the introduction of system and clarity into the framing of adequate standards of delegation; and the establishment of external auditing of agency policy making by an independent office of administrative procedure.

ADEQUATE STANDARDS OF DELEGATION

One of the important answers to the problem of administrative responsibility is periodic reexamination by the legislature of the standards of delegation and the manner in which statutory language has been interpreted in its administrative application. Reexamination could take the form of legislative studies of specific fields of law enforced by administrative agencies.

Another possible plan would require all legislative bills containing provisions authorizing agencies to grant or withhold licenses or similar types of consent—as well as bills containing express grants of rule-making authority—to include an appropriate indication thereof in their titles, and to have such bills receive special scrutiny by a designated legislative committee. Then the legislature would have the opportunity, before granting any authority, to decide (1) whether proper standards can be prescribed in the statutes and, if so, whether they have been stated; or (2) whether the agency should be required to prescribe its own standards; or (3) whether the regulatory authority being granted is so insignificant, or the need for unrestrained regulation so great, that the agency should be given discretion limited only by the most general of standards.[1]

There are certain kinds of policies that agencies should be permitted to make even though they are given no express policy-making authority by the statutory provisions relating to them. For example, the authority to make interpretative rules is implied in the very fact that an agency is required to administer the law. An agency must necessarily interpret statutory language in applying it to specific situations, and over a period of time it may develop general policies that it follows in its administration of the statute.[2] Also, when an agency has licensing or similar powers of granting or withholding consent, it is proper that it should develop forms and procedures to govern applications and other matters. And, finally, when an agency disposes of a large number of matters on the same basis, it naturally should develop certain general policies to guide it in making those decisions. Illustrative of this last type of policy are "policy bridges," discussed previously, which agencies should construct between general statutory standards and their case-by-case decisions.

A legislature should make clear, therefore, that agencies have

1 Helstad and Boyer, "Legislative Controls of Administrative Rule Making," pp. 1,048-51, at p. 1,050.
2 See Davis, *Administrative Law and Government* (1960), pp. 121-29.

authority to reduce such general policies to rule form and to promulgate, file, and publish them as rules, that they have authority to adopt such forms and procedures as they deem necessary for the administration of the law, and that they are free to make interpretative rules.

A provision in a general administrative procedure act expressly acknowledging that administrative agencies have these kinds of authority would confer no more authority on agencies than they already possess. Such a general provision would, however, make it clear that an agency has such authority and, consequently, that no agency—for fear of lack of authority—should hesitate to promulgate, file, and publish as rules its procedures, interpretations, and general policies. Wisconsin's administrative procedure act contains such a general provision.[3] The North Dakota provision authorizes each agency "to promulgate . . . reasonable rules . . . in conformity with the provisions of any statute administered . . . by such agency and to prescribe methods and procedures required in connection therewith. . . ."[4] The Minnesota provision is similar.[5]

AN OFFICE OF ADMINISTRATIVE PROCEDURE

Both the federal Attorney General's Committee on Administrative Procedure, which made its report in 1941 on federal procedures, and Robert M. Benjamin, who made his report in 1942 on administrative procedure in the state of New York, recommended the establishment of an agency that would work continually for the improvement of administrative procedure. No such agency has been created in New York, but one was established in California in 1945, and a small advisory office was created in the Department of Justice in 1957.

The Benjamin report.   Mr. Benjamin was impressed with the number and complexity of problems in the field of administrative procedure. He felt that the constant change occurring in this field

---

[3] Wis. Stat., sec. 227.014 (1955).
[4] N. Dak. Code, sec. 28-3203 (1943).
[5] Minn. Stat., sec. 15.042 (1) (1953).

necessitated continual attention on the part of some officer or agency. Moreover, he believed that many of the corrective measures he proposed were experimental and would require further study and observation. He recommended, therefore, that a division of administrative procedure be established to perform the following functions:

1. To continue permanently an objective and detailed examination and study of quasi-judicial and quasi-legislative procedures and of problems of judicial review.

2. To act as a source of technical information and expert assistance to the departments, boards and commissions of the State government with respect to their procedures.

3. To assist, on the request of an agency, in the preparation or revision of its procedural rules.

4. To receive from the public complaints and suggestions with respect to procedures that are considered objectionable or subject to improvement.

5. To assist in an advisory capacity in reconciling differences that arise out of conflicting or overlapping jurisdiction or procedures of different agencies.

6. To administer the legislation that must be enacted . . . to provide for the publication of rules and regulations.

7. To report to the Governor, annually or at more frequent intervals, on the results of its study and examination and on its other activity; such reports to include recommendations for any legislation that is thought to be desirable.[6]

The Attorney General's committee. Many of the same considerations that prompted Benjamin to recommend the establishment of a division of administrative procedure in New York induced the Attorney General's committee to recommend the establishment of a similar organization in the federal government. The committee's report states that:

The Committee has been impressed in the course of its inquiries not only by the need for dissimilarities in administrative procedures . . . but also by the possibilities for greater uniformity in many subordinate particulars. The Committee has also been much impressed by the absence in many agencies of information or interest concerning the procedures in other parts of the Federal administrative establishment.

6 Benjamin, *Administrative Adjudication in the State of New York*, p. 18.

These circumstances, especially when joined with others about to be mentioned, strongly suggest the desirability of establishing within the Federal Government a permanent organization to devote attention to the agencies' common procedural problems. True, the vigor of procedural reforms and the alteration of existing practices depend perhaps not so much on forces outside the agencies as on the agencies' own sensitivity to the need for self-criticism and improvement; nevertheless, improvements may well be stimulated by an organization especially qualified to perceive existing defects and suggest correctives.[7]

Office of Federal Administrative Procedure. Similar recommendations were made intermittently thereafter to establish such a federal unit.[8] Acting on these recommendations, the Attorney General in 1957 established the Office of Federal Administrative Procedure in the Department of Justice. His departmental order empowers the office to:

(a) Carry on continuous studies of the adequacy of the procedures by which Federal departments and agencies determine the rights, duties, and privileges of persons;

(b) Initiate cooperative effort among the departments and agencies

---

[7] Committee on Administrative Procedure, *Final Report of the Attorney General's Committee on Administrative Procedure*, p. 123.

[8] In 1949, the Commission on Organization of the Executive Branch of the Government (First Hoover Commission) recommended "that the Administrative Management Division of the Office of the Budget should, with the aid of carefully selected legal consultants, suggest ways and means to improve and thereby reduce the cost of disposing of business before administrative agencies" (H. Doc. 116, 81st Cong., 1st sess., pp. 10-11). In 1953, the President called a Conference on Administrative Procedure consisting of seventy-five members and delegates. After nearly two years of study, the conference made thirty-five recommendations concerning ways and means to improve administrative practice and procedure. Of two recommendations made to the President, the first was for the establishment of an office of administrative procedure in the Department of Justice under the supervision of the Attorney General (*Report of the Conference on Administrative Procedure* [Washington, D. C.: U. S. Gov't. Printing Office, 1955], recommendation A.1, pp. 3-4, and Comment, pp. 46-48). Subsequently, the Commission on Organization of the Executive Branch of the Government (Second Hoover Commission), in its report on legal services and procedure, made this recommendation: "An Office of Legal Service and Procedure should be established within the Department of Justice to assist agencies in simplifying, clarifying, and making uniform rules of substance and procedure; to insure agency compliance with statutory publication requirements; and to receive and investigate complaints regarding legal procedures and report thereon to the authorities concerned" (*Report of the Commission on Organization of the Executive Branch of the Government* [Washington, D. C.: U. S. Gov't. Printing Office, 1955], recommendation 49, p. 84).

and their respective bars to develop and adopt so far as practicable uniform rules of practice and procedure;

(c) Collect and publish facts and statistics concerning the procedures of the departments and agencies;

(d) Assist departments and agencies in the formulation and improvement of their administrative procedures.[9]

Having only experimental or interim status, the office is quite small, consisting of a director, two staff attorneys, and two secretaries. Its budget has totaled approximately $50,000 each year. Each of forty-eight departments and agencies has cooperated to the extent of designating an officer to maintain liaison with the office. In addition, the office staff meets informally with members of agency staffs having particular problems. The office also maintains contact with the administrative law sections of the American and Federal Bar Associations, and with other interested groups. Its director, John F. Cushman, described the functioning of the office as follows:

> To provide some indication of the workload of the Office, during the first year of operation it participated in 69 intradepartmental studies and assignments, 22 rulemaking studies affecting one or more departments and agencies, and processed 29 special assignments. Last year, it handled 117 assignments falling into the following general categories: 43 reviews of legislative proposals, 23 special assignments, 21 interagency studies and advisory opinions, 14 rulemaking proceedings, and 16 interagency conferences.
>
> The range of these assignments extends from study and advice with respect to possible change in one rule to the revision or preparation of rules for the conduct of agency hearings. They include assistance in the drafting of legislation and the providing of views on the form and legality of such proposals. It should be emphasized here that while no agency is required to seek our advice, and when sought it is advisory only, a most significant development, in my opinion, has been the frequency of requests for the services of the Office.[10]

9 Office of the Attorney General, Order No. 142-57, 22 *Federal Register* 998, February 6, 1957.

10 Statement of John F. Cushman, Director, Office of Administrative Procedure, Department of Justice, in *Administrative Procedure Legislation* (Washington, D. C.: U. S. Gov't. Printing Office), Hearings before the U. S. Senate Subcommittee on Administrative Practice and Procedure of the Committee on the Judiciary, 86th Cong., 1st sess., pursuant to S. Res. 61, July 21, 22, 23, 1959, and November 19, 20, 1959, pp. 213-14.

The office assumes no responsibilities concerning the receiving and handling of complaints or the publication of agency policies. As Mr. Cushman indicated, the office has advisory powers only.[11]

California's office. The California Department of Administrative Procedure was patterned after the proposals of the federal Attorney General's committee. Perhaps the major function of the Department is that of maintaining a qualified staff of independent hearing officers and assigning the officers to agencies requesting their services. The use of independent hearing officers is designed to secure some degree of separation of prosecuting and adjudicating functions within an agency.

The California Department is also directed to "study the subject of administrative law and procedure in all its aspects; to submit its suggestions to the various agencies in the interests of fairness, uniformity and the expedition of business; and to report its recommendations to the Governor and Legislature at the commencement of each general session." Pursuant to this directive, the Department issues biennial reports setting forth its observations and recommendations. For example, in its fourth biennial report, the Department recommended, among other things, the enactment of legislation to make it more difficult for agencies to circumvent rule-making procedural requirements through use of the emergency provision.

The function of supervising the publication of the California administrative code and register was transferred to the Department of Administrative Procedure in 1947. The Department prescribes the manner and form in which rules must be prepared, printed, and indexed, the numbering of rules, and the time of publishing the register, and also performs certain functions with respect to the filing of rules.[12]

---

11 *Ibid.*, p. 217. In his report to President-elect Kennedy in December 1960, James M. Landis recommended transfer of the functions of the office to the secretariat of his proposed permanent Conference of Administrative Procedure (*op. cit., supra,* Chapter 6, at note 15). In a special message to Congress, President Kennedy recommended establishment of such a conference (*New York Times,* April 14, 1961, p. 12).

12 Wisconsin Legislative Council, *1955 Report, Administrative Rule Making,* p. 185.

Advantages and disadvantages. The alleged advantages of an office of administrative procedure have already been mentioned. Such an office could act as a study or research center in the field of administrative law and procedure, as a vehicle for receiving complaints and for investigating meritorious ones, as an adviser to the various agencies on technical procedural problems, as a disseminator of relevant information among the agencies, as the supervisor of the rules publication system, as an adviser to the legislature and chief executive on legislation in the field of administrative procedure, and possibly as the supervisor of a staff of independent hearing officers, assuming that such a staff is established.

The disadvantages or limitations attributed to an office of administrative procedure were succinctly stated in Senate Document No. 248, 79th Congress, 2nd Session, dealing with the history of the Federal Administrative Procedure Act:

> It is objected that such an office—in addition to involving the creation of another administrative agency—will be political, will interfere with the independent operation of boards and commissions, will constitute a superadministrative agency, will serve to unduly emphasize and channel complaints respecting the administrative process, or will be without real authority.

Most of the fears expressed in these objections apparently have not materialized in the one jurisdiction that has had the most experience with an office of administrative procedure. California's experience seems to indicate that such an agency can perform substantial service in the field of administrative law and procedure without exerting the influences ascribed to it by its detractors.[13]

These objections can be precluded, for the most part, by making such an office completely independent of the executive branch and solely responsible to the legislature. There is precedent in the creation of the General Accounting Office in 1921. Congress assured the independence of the GAO by providing that its head, the Comptroller General, serve a fifteen-year term and that he be removed only by joint resolution of Congress upon cause.

[13] *Ibid*, p. 188.

It may be argued that if an office of administrative procedure is made responsible to the legislature rather than to the chief executive, it will not become either another administrative agency or a super-administrative agency within the executive branch. It will be, instead, a legislative agency. Justification for such an agency can be found in theoretical as well as practical considerations. It may be contended that since the legislature has constitutional power to make *all* laws, and its members feel increasingly impelled to control administrative policy making in order to stem the loss of, and hence retain, basic control of the lawmaking function, then an office established to audit administrative lawmaking and procedure should be made just as responsible to the legislature as an office established to audit administrative expenditures to help the legislature keep control of the purse strings. From the frames of reference of limited government and popular control, there is as much justification for legislative audit of administrative lawmaking as for legislative audit of administrative spending.

Accordingly, the director of an office of administrative procedure could be appointed for an extraordinary term of office, exceeding the terms of the chief executive and any legislator, with his removal effected only by resolution of the legislature upon cause. Thereby, he would be made less susceptible than all government officers, save judges, to political influence emanating from the executive branch, the legislature, or the public. This plan admittedly would be more feasible if the staff of hearing officers, if any, were made responsible to an officer of the executive branch—such as the Attorney General—rather than to the director of an independent office of administrative procedure. One may argue, however, that all other functions of the office could be exercised as well or better by an office responsible to the legislature rather than to the chief executive.

Conclusion. Such an independent office could be the legislature's primary instrument for assuring compliance of administrative agencies to general procedural legislation. It could report periodically to the legislature concerning incidents of noncompliance and make recommendations for new legislation to improve administrative procedure. It could conduct studies of specific fields of administrative law, or otherwise aid the legislature to conduct such studies, in order to effect more adequate and clear statutory standards of delegation of policy-making discretion. It could serve as the legislature's "watchdog" in ferreting out hidden agency policies or laws so that they are published as rules and made known to both legislators and affected members of the public. It could stimulate agencies to build bridges between case-by-case decisions and general statutory standards. It could supervise a rules publication system. It could advise agencies with respect to administrative procedure, stimulate their utilization of public participation devices in policy making where feasible, evaluate and investigate meritorious complaints, and generally act as a continuing and salutary influence toward improving administrative policy making. The results would be notable: helping the legislature to keep control of the lawmaking function; helping administrators to exercise responsibility within legislative intent; and helping to reduce the causes of legislative-administrative conflict.[14]

14 In 1958, the American Bar Association proposed legislation (S. 600) that would establish an "independent" office of administrative procedure. This proposal, among others, prompted creation of a new standing subcommittee of the Senate Judiciary Committee, the Subcommittee on Administrative Practice and Procedure (S. Res. 61, 86th Cong., 1st sess.). As proposed, S. 600 would provide for a director and deputy director of administrative practice to head the new office, the former to be appointed by the President with Senate consent for a ten-year term, and the deputy for a five-year term, both removable by the President "for inefficiency, neglect of duty, or malfeasance of office." The new office would assume all the duties and functions now exercised by the existing office in the Department of Justice, those exercised by the Administrator of General Services and the Federal Register Division under the Federal Register Act, and all the functions relating to trial examiner and hearing examiner positions within the jurisdiction of the Civil Service Commission. (Compare Landis' proposal, *supra*, Chapter 6, note 15.) The director would exercise vast powers over legal practice and procedures and an independent career service of "hearing commissioners" as well as other legal officers. The director would be required to report annually to Congress and the President, and as may be directed. Though the director's status would by no means be as "independent" of the executive branch as that of the Comptroller General, it is significant that the proposed legislation provides: "The Director, from time to time, shall submit recommendations directly to the Congress for additional legislation which he deems necessary or desirable for furthering the purposes of this Act." Morever, he is given considerable independence with regard to expenditures and housekeeping functions (*Administrative Procedure Legislation, op. cit., supra*, note 10, at pp. 2-20).

Chapter Eight

Implications
for
Administrative Theory

The five sequential stages of the policy-making cycle, though broadly identifiable, are not so discrete and simple as to preclude frequent elimination of one or more stages of the cycle. Even thus conceived, there are many exceptions, for *typical* policy making—with respect to details of the administrative process—simply does not exist in the context of our governmental pluralism.

CONCEPTUAL PROPOSITIONS

Nevertheless, in an idealized form the policy-making cycle is tantamount to the structure of a model. From this model, certain conceptual propositions emerge that have important implications for administrative theory:

1. Policy making in public administration is not devoid of an identifiable process capable of descriptive analysis.

2. This process consists of a cycle of five sequential stages—initiation, preliminary drafting, public participation, final drafting, and reviewing.

3. The most important stages substantively, and the most complex procedurally (those that involve the most participants) are the initiation and public participation stages.

4. The initiation and public participation stages involve the vital interaction of public administration with its external environment.

5. This vital interaction is organized and purposeful, rather than individual and accidental.

Insofar as the essential validity of these propositions has been, or can be, demonstrated by this description of the policy-making cycle, the following implications for administrative theory may be drawn: (1) Public administration needs to be redefined to reflect the essence and importance of agency policy making and its intrinsic environmental interaction. (2) This environmental interaction is similar in some respects to policy making in other large organizations. (3) The policy-making cycle in government agencies is compatible with a *general* theory of administration. (4) More specifically, the co-optative stages of policy making in public administration suggest a theory of *democratic* administration.

REDEFINITION OF PUBLIC ADMINISTRATION

Most students of public administration have discarded the old notion that administration in a government setting is distinct and separate from policy making.[1] Description of the policy-making cycle sup-

1 See, for example, Appleby, *Policy and Administration,* Chapter I; Murray Edelman, "Governmental Organization and Public Policy," *Public Administration Review,* XII (Autumn 1952), 276-83, at pp. 282-83; and Simon, Smithburg, and Thompson, *Public Administration,* pp. 428-29. But compare John Walton, *Administration and Policy Making in Education* (Baltimore: Johns Hopkins University Press, 1959). Not only does Walton assert that "a clear separation between policy formation and administrative action is essential," but he attempts to show that such a distinction is "theoretically sound" (*ibid.,* pp. 44-45). According to Walton, "the administrator [in education] is not a colorful figure engaged in innovations," and he makes the point that "originality and creativity, as well as conventional competence in intellectual matters are not likely to be considered particularly desirable in educational administrators" (*ibid.,* pp. 60, 62). One might respond to Mr. Walton that if his observations are true, as well they may be, then he may unwittingly have discovered what is basically wrong with the American educational system.

ports this conclusion. Policy making and administration are not only inseparable, they are indistinguishable in modern public administration. Indeed, a government agency has been defined as an organization that makes policy.[2] A modern conception of public administration, therefore, must not merely recognize the importance of agency policy making. We have reached a point in the evolution of bureaucracy when administration must be defined explicitly in terms of the importance of policy making.

The policy-making cycle implies, moreover, that any modern definition of public administration must make reference to the intrinsic character of the process of agency policy making. We have observed that both the first and third stages of the cycle—initiation and public participation—involve interaction between the organization and its external environment. The other three stages—making the preliminary and final drafts, and administrative review—involve interaction within the administrative network. Accordingly, though perhaps the statement verges toward a truism, the intrinsic character of agency policy making may be described as environmental interaction.

Furthermore, our descriptive analysis reveals that environmental interaction in policy formulation is purposeful and organized. It is purposeful, and not accidental, because an objective is being sought; the process is goal-oriented.[3] It is organized rather than individual because each of the five stages is characterized by the interaction, even the interdependence, of groups of persons. Rarely does any stage of the cycle involve exclusively the action of only one person.[4]

Finally, within the framework of limited government or a government of law, agency policy formulation is systematic. Though flexible, variable, and situational in its comprehensive dimensions, the process is not devoid of method and orderliness and is capable of description.

[2] Davis, *Administrative Law and Government* (1960), p. 11.

[3] "The assumption of purposeful behavior excludes . . . random responses having no value base" (Richard C. Snyder and Glenn D. Paige, "The United States Decision to Resist Aggression in Korea," *Administrative Science Quarterly*, III (December 1958), 341-78, at p. 345.

[4] "Official decision makers do not behave as discrete individuals but as participants or role players in an organizational system" (*ibid.*, p. 346).

The following, then, is suggested as a definition of public administration that incorporates the factors discussed:

Public administration is that organized and purposeful interaction of society which, within law, systematically formulates and applies policies of government agencies.

SIMILARITY WITH OTHER ORGANIZATIONS

James D. Thompson and William J. McEwen have developed two main lines of analysis that emphasize (1) the interdependence of complex organizations within the larger society and the consequences this has for organizational goal setting; (2) the similarities of goal-setting processes in organizations with manifestly different goals.[5]

If the term "policy making" is substituted for "goal setting," it follows that our description of agency policy making substantiates their first line of analysis so far as public administration is concerned. Their other emphasis requires further comment.

According to Thompson and McEwen, " a continuing situation of necessary interaction between an organization and its environment introduces an element of environmental control into the organization."[6] One of the principal means by which interaction may provide for environmental control over goal-setting decisions, they term "co-optation." In developing the similarity among large organizations in this respect, they borrow Philip Selznick's definition of co-optation as "the process of absorbing new elements into the leadership or policy-determining structure of an organization as a means of averting threats to its stability or existence."[7]

In terms of this line of reasoning, then, the policy-making process in government agencies is similar to the policy-making process in other organizations. Initiating agency policy making and eliciting public participation are stages that involve co-optation. These stages

[5] James D. Thompson and William J. McEwen, "Organizational Goals and Environment: Goal Setting as an Interaction Process," *American Sociological Review*, XXIII (February 1958), 23-31.

[6] *Ibid.*, pp. 24, 27-28.

[7] Selznick, *TVA and the Grass Roots*, p. 13.

of the process involve the kind of environmental impingement upon government agencies that effects changes in their policies. Some of this interaction is what Selznick terms "formal co-optation"—that is, "the establishment of openly avowed and formally ordered relationships."[8] Examples from our analysis are advisory committees and public hearings. Other interaction is "informal co-optation"—that is, "a response to the pressure of specific centers of power within the community."[9] Examples are informal conferences and consultations and the unstructured, but direct, contact of external stimulators with agency personnel through letter, telephone, or personal conversation. Initiation of most administrative policy making, we have observed, is by variable and informal means.

Regardless which type of co-optation is more important in the policy-making process of public administration, co-optation—to paraphrase Thompson and McEwen—is effective to the extent that it places the representative of an "outsider" in a position to determine the occasion for a policy decision, to participate in analyzing the existing situation, to suggest alternatives, and to take part in the deliberations of consequences.[10]

A GENERAL THEORY OF ADMINISTRATION

The similarity between policy making in government agencies and policy making in other organizations does not stop with co-optation. It becomes even more apparent when the policy-making cycle in government agencies and the administrative process generally are compared comprehensively.

The five sequential stages of agency policy making coincide with Edward H. Litchfield's major postulate that the administrative process is a cycle of action comprised of decision making, programming, communicating, controlling, and reappraising.[11] In an idealized

---

8 *Ibid.*
9 *Ibid.*, p. 14.
10 Thompson and McEwen, *op. cit.*, pp. 23-31, at p. 27.
11 Edward H. Litchfield, "Notes on a General Theory of Administration," *Administrative Science Quarterly*, I (June 1956), 2-29, at pp. 12-20.

form, he suggests, the process occurs as a logical sequence of progression from one phase to another, though often the process occurs in abbreviated form with the elimination of one or more phases. Reappraisal makes the process cyclical, for this phase brings the sequence back to, substantially, the point at which it began.[12]

Correlated with the Litchfield thesis, the present analysis of agency policy making appears as follows: (1) initiation (decision making); (2) preliminary drafting (programming); (3) public participation (communicating); (4) final drafting (controlling); (5) reviewing (reappraisal).

Accordingly, initiating an agency policy proposal involves the making of a decision—i.e., issue definition and the exercise of choice or discretion to proceed with policy formulation. Making the preliminary draft involves interpretation of the decision in the form of specific programs—i.e., the giving of at least tentative substance to the proposal in terms of agency objectives, purposes, and resources. Eliciting public participation through consultations, committees, and hearings involves communicating the programmed decision—i.e., transmitting stimuli between individuals or groups. Final drafting of the policy involves establishment of control for the realization of the decision—i.e., definition of the desired response and the methods of assuring its occurrence. And, finally, administrative review of the policy involves a reappraisal of the decision as programmed, communicated, and controlled—i.e., reappraisal necessitated not only by change from original facts, assumptions, and values, but by possible improvements made apparent by time and circumstance. We have observed, moreover, that the five sequential stages of agency policy making, though broadly identifiable, are not so discrete as to preclude frequent elimination of one or more stages of the process.

It is suggested, therefore, that our descriptive analysis of policy making in public administration lends further support to a general theory of administration as hypothesized by Litchfield.

12 *Ibid.*, pp. 13, 19-20. Supporting the Litchfield thesis, insofar as the administration of contract research is concerned, is Alan C. Rankin, "The Administration of Contract and Grant Research," *Administrative Science Quarterly*, I (December 1956), pp. 275-94.

CO-OPTATION AND DEMOCRATIC ADMINISTRATION

To demonstrate the compatibility of policy making in public administration with administrative theory generally is not to equate the policy making cycle with autocratic administration.

Students of public administration have belabored Alexander Pope's adage: "For Forms of Government, let fools contest; / Whate'er is best administered is best." The notion is widely accepted today that the form of government is crucial in distinguishing democratic from autocratic administration. Though Mussolini made the trains run on time, efficiency should not be the only criterion for good administration, it is argued. And then it is explained how the representative or democratic form of government conditions public administration to become democratic.

The difficulty with this argument is that it includes too much. Administration is often autocratic within democratic forms of government. Many newly emerging nations with democratic forms have autocratic administrative systems. Even within the Western democracies, some government agencies persist as autocratic microcosms.

If the form of government alone does not necessarily distinguish democratic from autocratic administration, then what does? The degree to which co-optation is involved in the process of agency policy making seems a plausible answer.

In one of his essays, Warner W. Stockberger characterized administration as tending primarily to become autocratic. Even democratic administration cannot survive without authoritative leadership and recognition of the right of the leader to exercise his authority. But democratic administration, observed Stockberger, differs from autocratic administration "not in the possession and *use* of authority, but in the *manner* and cooperative spirit in which it is used." He explained:

> In administration the democratic way provides for freedom of individual expression and, through cooperative effort, seeks to gain voluntary

compliance with those policies or procedures which majority opinion considers the most desirable.[13]

So far as the policy-making cycle is concerned, "freedom of individual expression" and "cooperative effort" are primarily reflected in the initiation and public participation stages of agency policy making. The degree to which these co-optative stages are apparent in policy making may determine whether a given government agency is democratic or autocratic in its administration. How "public" is public administration may depend on the extent to which the outside "publics" participate in the administrative process.

Viewed conversely, if an agency is continuously unreceptive to outside influences in policy initiation and is unwilling to elicit public participation to consider policy proposals, its procedures cannot be characterized as democratic. The *manner* in which it uses its authority is indistinguishable from autocratic administration despite the context of its form of government.

If co-optation is a requisite for democratic administration, then some form of public participation in administrative policy making is vital. Public participation accords with the elementary axiom that in a democracy the governed should have the opportunity to participate in their government, either personally or through their representatives.

No longer can there be validity in the contention that administrative policy making is not analogous to legislative activity—that legislators have almost unlimited discretion in their policy making, while the administrator's discretion is confined within limits prescribed by the legislature. Such exegesis becomes spurious in the face of the ever growing magnitude and importance of administrative policy making. To anyone who has examined the frequently broad delegations of policy-making authority to administrative agencies, the difference between the legislature's and the administrator's discretion is merely

[13] Warner W. Stockberger, *As I See It: Observations of a Civil Servant* (Washington, D. C.: U. S. Department of Agriculture Graduate School, 1941), p. 13.

one of degree rather than of kind.[14] The equation of public participation and democracy, therefore, is as relevant to policy making by
administrative agencies as it is to lawmaking by legislatures.

THE MANAGEMENT OF CONFLICT

We have concluded that if an agency is continuously unreceptive to
outside influences in policy making, its procedures cannot be characterized as democratic. In other words, without co-optation there cannot be democratic administration. But this is not the same as saying
that the mere presence of co-optation assures that administration is
democratic, for "it would be illusory to build a theory of administration upon the belief that the effective public in every instance consists
merely of those engaged directly."[15]

John Gaus posed the issue in this manner: "You will ask, really is
it the public that is participating or an anti-public ganging up of the
greedy, the sly, the selfish, or at best the narrow-minded, taking over
for their own benefit the powers . . . of government?"[16] What, then, is
the public to which government should be responsible? Though
Jeremy Bentham attributed no such evils to the public, is the public,
as he maintained, "the sum of the interests of the several members
who compose it"?[17] Or does the public comprise, as Edmund Burke

[14] "The content of regulations necessarily lies partly in the discretion of the
agency devising them, since the very reason for authorizing their issuance instead
of incorporating fixed rules in the governing statutes is to enable administrative
judgment to shape them. The permissible content of most regulations is subject to
great variation, with a multiplicity of choices lying within the limits of possibility . . ." (Ralph F. Fuchs, "The Model Act's Division of Administrative Proceedings
into Rule Making and Contested Cases," *Iowa Law Review*, XXXIII [January 1948],
210-27, at p. 221.

[15] John M. Gaus, "Public Participation in Federal Programs," in Conaway (ed.),
Democracy in Federal Administration, p. 16, quoting from a paper by Lane Lan-
caster cited as "Private Associations and Public Administration" (1934).

[16] *Ibid.*, p. 14.

[17] Jeremy Bentham, *An Introduction to the Principles of Morals and Legislation*,
Chapter I, section iv, in Edwin A. Burtt (ed.), *The English Philosophers from
Bacon to Mill* (New York: The Modern Library, 1939), p. 792.

stated and Walter Lippman applauded, "those who are living, those who are dead, those who are to be born"?[18]

This question has perplexed political scientists over the past generation. No one has examined the vast literature on the subject in greater detail than Glendon Schubert. After carefully analyzing the public-interest concepts of more than one hundred and fifty scholars, Schubert concluded that "there is no public-interest theory worthy of the name" and that "the public-interest concept makes no operational sense."[19]

When making policy decisions, therefore, it is doubtful that public administrators find practical utility in any concept of a public interest. What is important is that the conflict inherent in the politics of policy making be managed—that the relationship between an agency and its task environment be controlled. Thus, James D. Thompson has observed that "to the extent that the organization can choose between various postures relative to the task environment, it can manage conflict stemming from competing pressures." By "task environment" he was not referring to the total community, society, or public, but to those parts of it that are not indifferent to the organization. By organizational "posture" he meant the relationship between an organization and its task environment. According to Thompson, organizational posture depends upon the distinctiveness or prestige of the personnel of the organization and the nature of their exposure to the task environment. Though he recognized that an organization does not always have full control over its posture, it can affect its relationship by controlling its members' identification and interaction with, and their exposure to, the environment. When members interact regularly with the same elements of the task environment, their identification with the organization tends to become eroded. The more members exposed, moreover, the more directions in which loyalties are pulled, and the more varied are the kinds and

18 Walter Lippman, *The Public Philosophy* (New York, Mentor Books, 1955), p. 35.
19 Glendon Schubert, *The Public Interest, A Critique of the Theory of A Political Concept* (Glencoe, Ill.: The Free Press, 1960), pp. 223, 224.

numbers of problems the organization faces. Thompson concluded: "Thus by varying the distinctiveness of the organization, the proportion of members exposed, and the frequency and regularity of their exposure, the organization gains a measure of control over conflict stemming from potential reactions to competing pressures."[20]

In other words, in order to manage conflict in policy formation, an agency administrator must maintain control over his organization so that its relationships with its total environment may, in turn, be managed. To make qualitative policy decisions, public administration should continually strive to improve the methods and conditions of these relationships. In his classic, *The Public and its Problems,* John Dewey asserted that such improvement "depends essentially upon freeing and perfecting the processes of inquiry and of dissemination of their conclusions." And he concluded: "That is *the* problem of the public."[21]

CONCLUSION

The quest for legislative devices to control administrative policy making appears to be nationwide. Insofar as an administrative procedure act prescribes reasonable and enforceable minimum requirements for administrative agencies of a jurisdiction to follow in their policy making, greater administrative responsibility is likely. Legislatively prescribed principles of equity and justice need not fetter administrative discretion unreasonably in their application—as, for example, uniform requirements for rules publication, for holding and conducting of public hearings, or for the attainment of judical review. Such requirements represent attempts by legislatures to maintain an increased measure of control over lawmaking by administrators. Lawmaking by administrative agencies need not be incompatible with the fundamental principles of our system of government so long

---

[20] Thompson, "Organizational Management of Conflict," pp. 389-409, especially pp. 394-96. For the relationship of organizational prestige to organizational dependency, see Charles Perrow, "Organizational Prestige: Some Functions and Dysfunctions," *American Journal of Sociology,* LXVI (January 1961), 335-41.

[21] Dewey, *The Public and Its Problems,* p. 208.

as legislatures retain basic control of the process of administrative policy making.

In recognizing that the rise of administrative agencies has been the most significant legal trend of this century, the late Justice Jackson of the United States Supreme Court observed in 1952 that "perhaps more values today are affected by their decisions than by all the courts."[22] And another eminent jurist, Arthur T. Vanderbilt, declared in 1947 that agency legislation had already exceeded in volume "by many times the corresponding additions to the statute books."[23]

What the future will bring is a matter of speculation, of course. It would seem that one may expect technological, economic, and social changes of great moment, with consequent problems posed for government. Necessity will continue to dictate increased delegation. Bureaucracy will continue to burgeon. Legislatures will become more frustrated in their attempts to cope with these problems. The dilemma confronting legislatures will grow in all its dimensions, and the chasm so apparent now between the legislative process and administrative policy making will deepen, unless reasonable and workable accommodations between the two are effected. Otherwise, government in the United States is destined to drift either toward chaos or major constitutional, structural, and political surgery. Either alternative could exact a high price in individual liberty and democracy. Meanwhile, bureaucracy in America will remain on trial.

---

22 Federal Trade Commission v. Ruberoid Co., 343 U. S. 470, 486 (1952).

23 Arthur T. Vanderbilt, in George Warren (ed.), *The Federal Administrative Procedure Act and Administrative Agencies* (New York: New York University Press, 1947), p. iii.

Index